BEHIND CLOSED DOORS

Secrecy in the International Financial Institutions

edited by Catherine Musuva

2006

© IDASA and the Global Transparency Initiative 2006

ISBN 1-920118-21-7

ISBN-13: 978-1-920118-21-1

6 Spin St
Cape Town, South Africa
8001

Cnr Prinsloo and Visagie Streets
P.O Box 56950
Arcadia 0007
Pretoria
South Africa

Websites:
www.idasa.org
www.ifitransparency.org

Editing: Moira Levy, IDASA Publishing
Design: Valerie Phipps-Smith, Double Image Studios
Cover design: Valerie Phipps-Smith, Double Image Studios

Table of contents

Acknowledgments

I would like to acknowledge with great appreciation the following: Jennifer Kalafut (Bank Information Centre) for her guidance in formulating the requests for information; Thomas Carson (consultant to Open Society Justice Initiative) for analysis and technical support, the Open Society Justice Initiative for the initial methodology and software; Richard Calland (IDASA) and Toby McIntosh (Freedominfo) for reviewing and enriching the report with their input; the country co-ordinators: Victor Ricco, Paula Granada and Angeles Pereira (CEDHA); Nikolay Marekov (Access to Information Programme); Issa Luna Pla (LIMAC) and Peter Mihok (Friends of the Earth-CEPA); and all participating organisations in the five countries.

List of acronyms

AfDB	African Development Bank
AIP	Access to Information Programme
APIA	Access to Public Information Act
CAF	Andean Development Corporation
CAS	Country Assistance Strategy
CEDHA	Centre for Human Rights and Environment
CEPA	Centre for Environmental Public Advocacy
EBRD	European Bank for Reconstruction and Development
EIA	Environmental Impact Assessment
EIB	European Investment Bank
FOIA	Freedom of Information Act
FONPLATA	Financial Fund for the Development of the Rio de la Plata Basin
GEF	Global Environment Facility
GIS	Government Information Service
GTI	Global Transparency Initiative
IADB	Inter American Development Bank
IBRD	International Bank for Reconstruction and Development
ICP	Information, Consultation and Participation
IDASA	Institute for Democracy in South Africa
IDEAS	Institute for Educational Development and Social Action
IFC	International Finance Corporation
IFI	International Financial Institution
IIRSA	Integration of South American Regional Infrastructure
IMF	International Monetary Fund
ISPA	Instrument for Structural Policies for Pre-Accession
LFTAIP	Federal Transparency and Access to Public Government Information Law
LIMAC	Freedom of Information Mexico
NHWC	National Hazardous Waste Center
ODAC	Open Democracy Advice Centre
PAIA	Promotion of Access to Information Act
PAL	Programme Adjustment Loans
PCIA	Protection of Classified Information Act
PIC	Public Information Centre
PPDA	Protection of Personal Data Act
SANParks	South African National Parks

Executive summary

INTERNATIONAL FINANCIAL INSTITUTIONS (IFIs) wield significant power and influence – but it seems they do so mostly in secret. IFIs enter into agreements with borrowing governments which bind populations to terms and conditions which they are almost entirely unaware of. They mostly do so Behind Closed Doors. As this ground-breaking study of IFIs in five countries proves, obtaining IFI information is very difficult and only one in five requests for access to information is likely to penetrate the opacity of IFIs. Even though the IFIs publish copious volumes of operational information, more often than not, affected people are excluded from participating in decision-making processes and critical phases of the project cycle.

At national level, there have been great advances towards transparency and a meaningful public right to know in recent years. The IFIs are lagging. IFI information disclosure policies provide the framework for sharing information with the public about the activities of IFIs and are a demonstration of their commitment to transparency. However, these policies are applied inconsistently and lack adequate procedures for promoting the public's right to know. An opportunity is being squandered. Domestic Freedom of Information legislation in the countries where IFIs operate provide a more effective avenue for accessing public information held by government bodies. Transparency and accountability are fundamental requirements of good governance and democracy in the IFIs and because of the power and influence they wield, IFIs have human rights obligations to the populations they affect.

Though public, IFIs often have private sector operations, which in terms of information disclosure present a challenge in creating the right balance between confidentiality and presumption of disclosure. The transition from concealment to disclosure requires a strengthening of the existing norms and procedures for public access to documents generated and held by IFIs. This goes hand in hand with investment in human infrastructure and a commitment to implementation.

These are the main findings of a study to monitor public access to information held by IFIs and natio-nal institutions conducted in 2005 in Argentina, Bulgaria, Mexico, Slovakia and South Africa. The five-country study is a project of the Global Transparency Initiative (GTI) aimed at promoting transparency and accountability in the IFIs.[1] The study was led by the Institute for Democracy in South Africa (IDASA) and brought together a total of nine civil society organisations in the five countries to participate in the study. One hundred and twenty requests for information, twenty four in each country, were submitted to IFIs and national bodies.

The requests were for two main categories of information: documents regarding institutional and policy decisions and documents related to specific projects in the five countries. Examples of the former include summaries of Board Meetings and discussions of Country Assistance Strategies. Examples of the latter include loan contracts and Environmental Impact Assessments.

The IFIs which received requests were the:
- African Development Bank;
- Andean Development Corporation;
- European Bank for Reconstruction and Development;
- European Investment Bank;
- Inter-American Development Bank;
- International Bank for Reconstruction and Development and International Finance Corporation of the World Bank Group;
- International Monetary Fund.

Relevant national bodies expected to hold the documents requested from IFIs also received the same requests.

Overall, only twenty-two per cent of information requests resulted in full disclosure. Eight per cent of the requests resulted in incomplete disclosure. Broken down by country, in Argentina six requests in Argentina, fourteen in Bulgaria, five in Mexico, eleven in Slovakia and seven in South Africa resulted in disclosure of different degrees.

The results showed:
- A generally high level of opacity surrounding the disclosure of information related to IFIs;
- Incidences of low quality of information

disclosure (with cases of incomplete information being provided with minimal detail), delays and other practical obstacles to disclosure;

❖ A lack of responsiveness in dealing with requesters and a poor commitment to promoting the right to know, with a substantial proportion of requests simply being ignored;

❖ Inconsistencies in the interpretation and application of disclosure policies resulting in different outcomes for the same requests in different countries;

❖ Inadequate communication and information sharing between IFIs and borrowing governments and centralisation of decision-making regarding information disclosure in the IFI headquarters;

❖ Freedom of Information Acts (FOIAs) provide an alternative avenue for access to IFI information but domestic implementation challenges persist and strict internal procedures are necessary;

❖ Bulgaria had the highest success rate in getting information but Slovakia produced standard-setting practices in FOIA implementation.

Performance was generally poor in Argentina, Mexico and Slovakia;

❖ The World Bank emerged as the most responsive IFI and corrective measures have been embraced by the Inter American Development Bank (IADB) office in Argentina and public bodies to improve transparency and accountability following the results of this study

This report contains details of the findings. It begins with an overview of the study objectives and the methodology. Thereafter, general results are analysed. This is followed by country case studies which offer insights into the local context; provide detailed results of the requested documents and the performance of the institutions; explain the challenges experienced and offer recommendations. The report concludes with a summary of the main findings and a set of recommendations for reform. The results show that the need for reform cannot be under-stated. This report is intended to be useful to individuals and groups committed to promoting transparency and accountability in public national and international institutions.

I. Introduction and methodology

THIS REPORT PRESENTS the findings of a co-ordinated series of requests for information submitted in 2005 by the Global Transparency Initiative (GTI) to public International Financial Institutions (IFIs) and national government agencies operating in Argentina, Bulgaria, Mexico, Slovakia and South Africa.[2] IFIs enter into binding agreements with borrowing governments which bind citizens to terms and conditions which they are almost entirely unaware of. The GTI believes that people have a right to information from these institutions and a right to participate in the development of policies that affect their lives. The democratic deficit surrounding public IFIs, characterised by a lack of transparency and accountability, together with the need for reform, stimulated the study.

THE STUDY, ONE among other activities of the GTI aimed at promoting transparency and accountability in the IFIs, was led by the Institute for Democracy in South Africa (IDASA). It was conducted with the following six objectives:

◆ To test IFI information disclosure policies and national Freedom of Information Acts (FOIAs);

◆ To shed light on and push the boundaries of IFI disclosure policies;

◆ To promote best practices in order to harmonise country standards upwards;

◆ To shed light on the relationships between IFIs and borrower governments;

◆ To provide a specific campaign to promote the active use of national FOIAs;

◆ To build relationships with like-minded organisations.

A total of one hundred and twenty requests, twenty-four in each country, were submitted by nine organisations using an adopted version of a standardised methodology developed by the Open Society Justice Initiative for evaluating freedom of information in different countries. In a two-phased process, requests were first submitted to the IFIs and a month later requests for the same documents were submitted to local institutions. Requests were then tracked across a representative selection of institutions, without their prior knowledge, in a realistic fashion that would not compromise the results.

Once the outcomes of the requests were clear, where possible interviews were held with officials of these institutions to inform them about the study, assess the internal procedures for providing information and discuss any issues arising from the study.

Some of the requests were exactly the same in all countries so as to provide a strong comparative dimension to the study. These were requests for general institutional and policy documents. Examples include summaries of Board of Directors' meetings. The rest were specific to the different countries – permitting participating organisations to request information that was of interest to them in the local context. Project-related documents such as loan contracts and project reports were requested. In addition, information was requested on public consultation processes of the IFIs, for example, in the processes for developing Country Assistance Strategies (CASs) and reviewing information disclosure policies. Details of all the requests are contained in Annex I. The requests were submitted by post, e-mail and in person to Information Officers, or the equivalent, where this information was available. A two-month response time-frame was given for requests submitted to IFIs. For the requests submitted to public national institutions the response time-frame was as set out by the domestic FOIA.

An effort was made to include organisations that are active in campaigning for full accountability in the IFIs and those active in campaigning for the right to know at the national level. This mix also reflects the constituency of the GTI. Two of the organisations which participated were founding organisations of the GTI and led the process in their respective countries IDASA and Freedom of Information Mexico (LIMAC). Three other organisations were selected to lead the process in the other countries, the Centre for Human Rights and Environment (CEDHA), Access to Information Programme (AIP) and the Centre for Environmental Public Advocacy (CEPA). All these organisations were required to consult with local groups in formulating the country-specific requests and identify a local counterpart to submit requests alongside them. The table below shows the organisations that participated in the study.

Table 1: List of organisations that participated in the GTI study

Country	Organisation
Argentina	Centre for Human Rights and Environment (CEDHA) Institute for Educational Development and Social Action (IDEAS)
Bulgaria	Access to Information Programme (AIP) CEE Bankwatch Network, Bulgaria
Mexico	Freedom of Information, Mexico (LIMAC)
Slovakia	Friends of the Earth – Centre for Environmental Public Advocacy (CEPA) Uplift
South Africa	Institute for Democracy in South Africa (IDASA) Open Democracy Advice Centre (ODAC)

In all the five countries, with the exception of Argentina, the right to information is enshrined in national law, summarised in the table below. In Argentina, provincial legislation exists, however at the national level there is only a decree that regulates access to information. These laws contain wide provisions and mechanisms for access to information held by government, which includes IFI-related information and set out a response time-frame of between ten and thirty working days. Effective implementation of these FOIAs is hampered, however, by in-country obstacles which are described later in the country case studies.

Though different in size, scope, areas of operation and policy, the IFIs wield significant power and influence. Though public, often they have private

Table 2: Freedom of information legislation in the five countries

Country	Legislation	Year
Argentina	Law on Access to Public Information in the Province of Cordoba	1999
Bulgaria	Access to Public Information Act	2000
Mexico	Federal Transparency and Access to Public Government Information Law	2002
Slovakia	Act on Free Access to Information	2000
South Africa	Promotion of Access to Information Act	2000

sector operations, which in terms of information disclosure present a challenge in creating the right balance between confidentiality and presumption of disclosure. Even though the IFIs publish copious volumes of operational information, the public does not have access to the most sensitive facts regarding actual decision-making processes.[3] The contents of IFI information disclosure policies are a strong indicator of their commitment to transparency. These policies, which dictate the terms for access to information held by the IFIs, are reviewed every three to four years with the aim of making more information available to the public. Some encouraging steps have been made. However, much more needs to be done to meet the same standards of openness as domestic governments prescribed in FOIAs. The GTI Transparency Charter[4] is one response to this. The Charter sets out ten standards and norms that govern IFI disclosure policies and the principles that should guide its practice.

An overview of the results of the co-ordinated requests for information is presented in the next section. This is followed by country-specific chapters which provide detailed results and analyses. All country reports follow a similar structure and also include a set of conclusions and recommendations. The last section of this report ties together the general conclusions drawn from the study and offers recommendations that are linked to the GTI Charter principles for change. It is hoped that the contents of this report will not only reveal a number of challenges in accessing IFI-related information but that they will also form a basis for dialogue between IFI watchers, activists and researchers on the one hand, and officials of the IFIs and national government on the other.

2. Overall results of the GTI study

The overall outcomes of the requests are presented in the chart below.

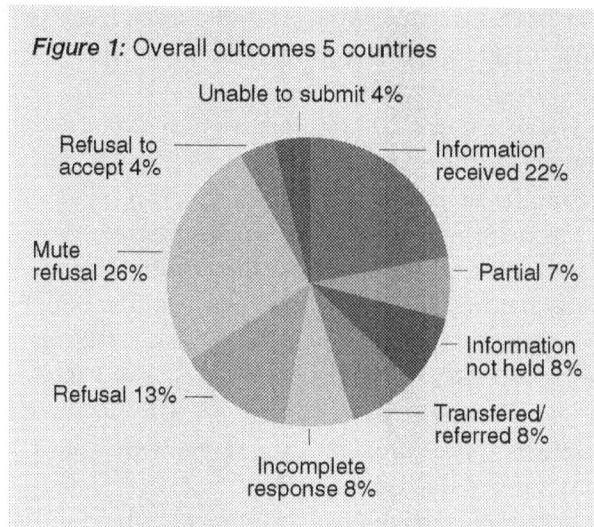

Figure 1: Overall outcomes 5 countries

Unable to submit 4%

Refusal to accept 4%

Information received 22%

Mute refusal 26%

Partial 7%

Information not held 8%

Refusal 13%

Transfered/ referred 8%

Incomplete response 8%

DESPITE THE EXISTENCE of IFI information disclosure policies and domestic FOIAs, obtaining IFI information is very difficult. Only 22 per cent of the 120 requests resulted in information being provided to the satisfaction of the requester, demonstrating the high walls of secrecy that surround information related to IFIs and their projects. Some of the documents which were disclosed were Environmental Impact Assessments for specific projects, project reports and summaries of meetings. Incomplete information was provided in eight per cent of the requests showing that information quality is compromised.

Non-disclosure of information was justified in writing in just thirteen per cent of the refusals. The results revealed a lack of responsiveness in dealing with requests shown by the high rate of 'mute refusals'[5] at twenty-six per cent. Where there is evidence that an institution received a request for information, a mute refusal is considered a violation of the FOIA. IFI disclosure policies on the other hand do not place an obligation to ever respond to a request. No appeals were lodged in the pilot study but the findings bring to the fore the need to enforce compliance with FOIAs – in the IFIs this could be initiated by establishing reasonable timeframes for responding to requests and appropriate mechanisms to ensure compliance.

The reasons for mute refusals differed from country to country but the main concern is that in these cases the information was not provided and no formal justification was ever given. In South Africa for instance, a government institution admitted that it had the information but preferred that the information be requested directly from the World Bank and did not provide the requester with a proper response. Legal grounding of refusals needs to become the norm where information cannot be disclosed. The country chapters that follow in this report probe the monitoring process from the requesters' point of view and illustrate that the experience of a requester will vary greatly from country to country and from IFI to IFI.

Although submitting a request should be a straightforward process if the receiving office is known, four per cent of the formulated requests could not be submitted despite several attempts. In addition, there was an institution which refused to accept a request for information from the requester. These peculiarities were only experienced in Argentina and are described in the country chapter.

Only twenty-two per cent of the 120 requests resulted in information being provided to the satisfaction of the requester, demonstrating the high walls of secrecy that surround information related to IFIs and their projects.

Eight per cent of all requests were either referred or transferred. Government agencies either referred the requests to IFIs or to other government agencies, while IFIs referred requests to government agencies which were said to hold the information. This outcome together with the eight per cent of requests where the requested information was not held were accepted in good faith and no further investigation was conducted to ascertain the claims put forward by the institutions. However, the fact that these requests did not result in the disclosure of information could imply that institutions can simply transfer or refer a request even when they have the information so as to impede access to the information.

Definitions of all the outcomes are contained in Annex II. A breakdown of the outcomes by country is provided in Annex III.

Testing IFI and national disclosure mechanisms for identical requests

Fifty-five paired requests were jointly submitted to various IFIs and national government bodies. Performance is rated highest in those outcomes where the information was provided (or partially provided). Refusals are rated lower and failures to respond (mute refusals or cases where the requester was unable to submit the request), receive the lowest rating. The performance of IFIs versus national bodies provided a comparative element and the results are presented below:

Overall, across all fifty-five cases of identical requests, in:
- Twenty-five per cent of the cases IFIs performed better than the national governments;
- Thirty-three per cent of the cases, national governments performed better;
- Forty-two per cent of the cases, both institutions performed in a similar manner.

In twenty-three cases, both institutions performed in the same manner. However, in only five of these cases, the final result was a positive outcome and the requested information was received. In another eight cases in which both institutions performed

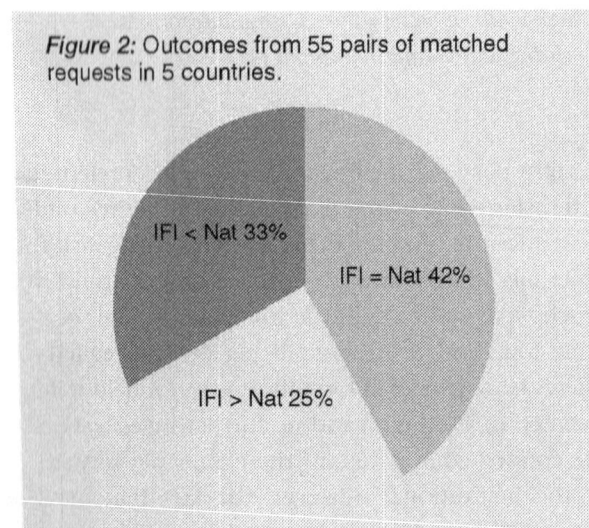

Figure 2: Outcomes from 55 pairs of matched requests in 5 countries.

the same, the final result was negative and no information was received. The requests were refused or transferred or referred away. In the remaining ten cases, both the IFI and the national institution failed to respond or accept the request in the first place.

In other words, when IFIs perform as well as national governments, in terms of compliance with their disclosure obligations, they are more likely to refuse or ignore the request than to provide the requested information.

The performance of IFIs relative to national governments is inconsistent among the different countries in the study. (See Table 3 opposite page)

IFIs perform as well as national governments in Bulgaria, the Slovak Republic and South Africa. In nearly half of the cases in which IFIs and national government institutions perform the same, the outcome is positive in Bulgaria and the Slovak Republic. The opposite is true for South Africa. In the three cases where the outcome is the same, both institutions ignored the request.

In Mexico, the national government outperforms the IFIs. The opposite is found in Argentina. The IFIs perform slightly better than the national government institutions. In the six cases where the outcome is the same, both institutions ignored the request.

Scope and limitations of IFI disclosure

The number of requests received varied from IFI to IFI. The African Development Bank (AfDB) received the lowest number of requests due to the participation of only one African country. The World Bank Group institutions the International Bank for Reconstruction and Development (IBRD) and International Finance Corporation (IFC) received the highest number of requests by virtue of the wide range of projects they fund in the five countries. Due to this, it is not possible to rank the IFIs. Of importance was how the different institutions responded to the requests they received, in general, and how they dealt with the standard requests, in particular.

Figure 3 on pg 5 shows a breakdown of the outcomes of all requests submitted to IFIs and national departments. Each IFI is singled out but all national government requests have been lumped together for the purpose of highlighting the IFIs' results.

A comparison of how IFIs responded to the standard requests submitted in each country showed discrepancy in the results.[6] Two requests were sub-

Table 3: Outcomes of matched requests by country

	Argentina	Bulgaria	Mexico	Slovak Rep.	S. Africa	Total
IFI > Nat	3	3	1	3	4	14
IFI < Nat	2	3	6	3	4	18
IFI = Nat	6	5	4	5	3	23
Total	11	11	11	11	11	55

In Argentina and Bulgaria these documents were disclosed by the World Bank but denied in Mexico, Slovakia and South Africa, showing inconsistency in interpreting the disclosure policy.

mitted to the World Bank requesting Summary of Board Meetings on the World Bank Disclosure Policy: Additional Issues, November 18, 2004 and the latest written statement presented to the Board from the Country Executive Director on the meeting where the present CAS was discussed. In Argentina and Bulgaria these documents were disclosed by the World Bank but denied in Mexico, Slovakia and South Africa, showing inconsistency in interpreting the disclosure policy. The refusals in the three countries were justified by clauses in the information policy which stated that these documents formed part of Board proceedings and as a result could not be disclosed. The fact that the documents were disclosed in some cases but not in others already raises questions about the classification of information

as confidential. It is in this vein that the GTI is campaigning for IFIs to open up all meetings with decision-making powers to the public. Inconsistencies were also observed in IMF disclosure. Standard requests were submitted for: minutes of discussion at the latest meeting of the Executive Directors of the IMF and concluding statements of Article IV missions, as well as a full schedule of upcoming missions. While efforts to submit these requests in Argentina and Mexico did not succeed, minutes were disclosed in Bulgaria and South Africa (and were available on the website). In Slovakia a short response stating that in effect minutes of meetings are not shared was provided. Regarding the upcoming country missions, the IMF was vague. A typical response to a request from the IMF states that all publicly available information is on the website and is accompanied by a weblink. Although posting information facilitates access to readily available information without the need to make a request, such a statement implies that information that is not on the website is not public and that a request for information that is not on the website will not result in

Figure 3: Results by institution type

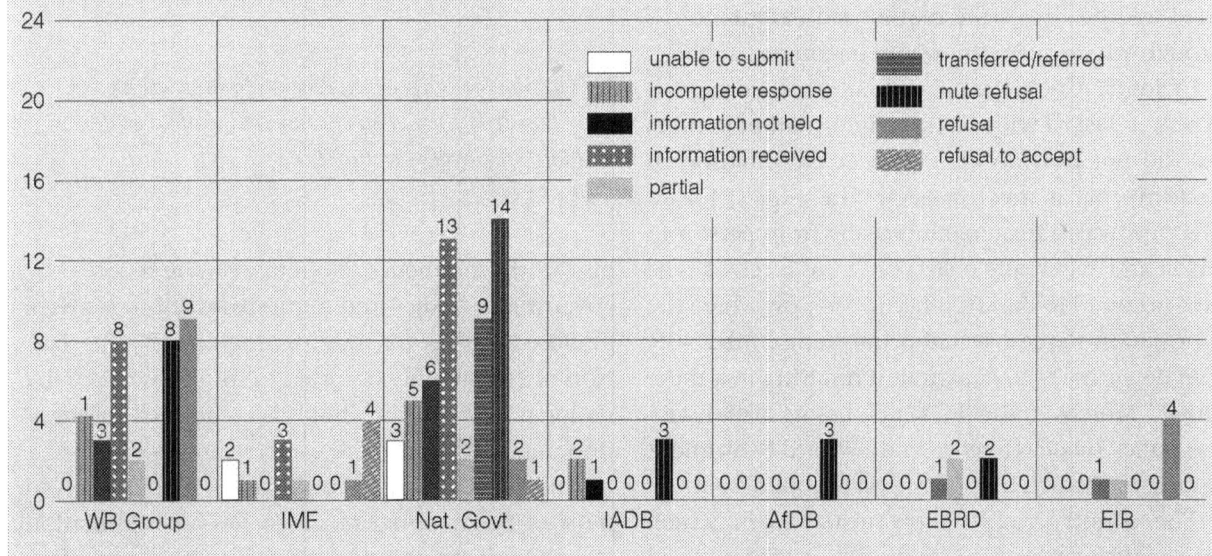

The fact that the documents were disclosed in some cases but not in others already raises questions about the classification of information as confidential. It is in this vein that the GTI is campaigning for IFIs to open up all meetings with decision-making powers to the public.

disclosure. The IMF therefore obfuscates what categories of information are available to the public.

Instead of providing legal grounds for non-disclosure, the European Investment Bank (EIB) shifts decisions for disclosure of loan agreements to national governments. Requests for project-related loan agreements in Bulgaria, Slovakia and South Africa therefore resulted in refusals.

IFIs compromised the quality of information by not providing information in the form that it was requested. In Bulgaria, requests for documents in Bulgarian resulted in English documents being disclosed because the documents did not exist in Bulgarian. Requests for copies of documents resulted in weblinks passing on the task of looking for this information to the requester. This was a typical response of the IMF as stated elsewhere in this report.

The IFC appears not to have a clear 'road map' for submission and handling of requests, a basic requirement in a disclosure policy. A 'road map' explains to the requester where a request should be submitted. It should indicate the office that receives requests and the designated official who receives requests. A full physical address and contact details including a telephone and fax number, as well as an email address, gives the requester different means through which they can submit a request.

In South Africa, the IFC did not have a designated person tasked with access to information matters and did not provide the requested information in the form that it was requested. The request for an interview was transferred internally from person to person and eventually no response was received. The same occurred in the IFC office in Moscow where the information request was also transferred internally from department to department resulting in a mute refusal.[7] Moreover, the IFC which has its own disclosure policy made reference to the World Bank and it was unclear which disclosure policy applies to it.

The country results show instances in which documents were denied by the IFIs, such as World

Bank Aide Memoires and loan contracts, but were disclosed by national government under FOIAs. This, together with the inconsistencies in the responses of the IFIs described above, point to limitations of the IFI disclosure policies and the need for reform. The study also revealed that some of the IFIs are making encouraging steps towards reform.

The Inter American Development Bank (IADB) office in Argentina requested CEDHA's collaboration to work on a document intended to enhance and optimise compliance with its information disclosure policy, in relation to time-frames and information quality. Similarly, the IADB Public Information Centre in Buenos Aires is keen on establishing a more active exchange with civil society.

The World Bank office in Slovakia would not disclose Aide Memoires relating to their internal character but did provide the requester with legal options, and offered support in initiating the procedure with the Slovak Government towards releasing Aide Memoire documents for projects.

Best practices in FOIA implementation

Implementation of FOIAs is not without its challenges as demonstrated by the low rate of information disclosure and conversely, the high rate of mute refusals, particularly in Argentina and South Africa. Nonetheless, Bulgaria and Slovakia had high success rates with national institutions. The Slovak FOIA emerged as a best practice case. Not only is there a strict and well drafted FOIA, which requires disclosure of every document that is not confidential according to the FOIA or any other law, but it

The Slovak FOIA emerged as a best practice case. Not only is there a strict and well drafted FOIA, but it also works in practice.

also works in practice. No refusals were reported by government bodies and requested documents were disclosed within ten days as required by the law. Non-disclosure only occurred in instances where the national body did not hold the requested information, meaning that there was nothing to disclose.

The Slovak Ministry of Finance, which received most of the national requests, has an Information Department made up of only five staff, including the Director and the webmaster. The Ministry has an internal policy which requires that requests are forwarded to the relevant department within a day of receiving the request. Any deemed refusals must be accompanied by legal reasons. The Ministry also pro-actively discloses information on its website and posts draft loan contracts with IFIs several weeks before they are signed for the public to comment. In order to accommodate the needs of different requesters, it continues to keep its old website running for those who were accustomed to searching for information on it even after developing a new, revamped website. Above all, the staff consider transparency as critical to citizens in realising their rights and to themselves in ensuring good work ethics.

This commitment to open practice translates to good performance of the Slovak FOIA and goes to show that political will and commitment are critical to the successful implementation of the law, no matter how good it may be on paper.

Relationships between IFIs and borrower governments

There were instances where government agencies implementing projects with IFIs did not possess project-related information as this information was being held by the IFIs. In Argentina, an official attributed delays in dealing with the IADB requests to not having the information from the IFI. He said that the project number had been changed by the IFI when the government took up the loan and the project could not be identified because it was classified under a different number.

In Slovakia, the Ministry of Finance did not have minutes of meetings, nor statements of foreign officials representing Slovakia in IFI governing bodies. The EIB did not provide the Ministry of Environment with the Environmental Impact Assessment it had conducted for one of its projects. Requests for information regarding reviews of strategic documents such as the CAS, which are an opportunity for public participation, were not responded to in detail by the EIB and the Ministry was not updated on this.

In South Africa, the Ministry of Finance made it clear that as a matter of procedure it had to consult with the respective IFIs before disclosing any IFI information. This was given as the main reason for the delay in responding to the requester. By the time of writing, the consultations had not led to dis-

closure. The Department of Environmental Affairs and Tourism evaded a request submitted to it, insisting that the request be submitted directly to the World Bank even after admitting that the Department had the information. If the document originated with the World Bank, there is a provision in the FOIA to issue a third party notice to the requester before determining whether or not to disclose the document. The Department failed to make use of this provision.

FOIAs as a tool for obtaining IFI information

Domestic FOIAs contain more detailed provisions and regulated mechanisms to access information than IFI information disclosure policies and therefore present an alternative route to obtaining IFI information. Even though the results demonstrate that in most countries government officials are not diligent in responding to requests, legal action can be taken against them, which is not the case with IFIs. Access to justice mechanisms through appeal structures therefore need to be tested in future work.

Even so, the study was able to demonstrate some successes in obtaining IFI information which was not disclosed by the IFI.

The Slovak FOIA resulted in faster and greater disclosure of IFI information. Presumption of disclosure is clearly spelled out in the Slovak FOIA for documents which are created by the Slovak institutions but is also applied for documents such as loan agreements with IFIs even though the EIB considers loan contracts confidential and refuses to disclose them. The legal analysis done by the Ministry of Finance did not find the loan agreement to be grounded sufficiently by the legal acts and therefore fully respected the presumption of disclosure principle.

The South African FOIA resulted in the disclosure of Aide Memoires for one project by South African National Parks (SANParks), which under the World Bank policy were confidential. Other World Bank documents were disclosed albeit in controversial circumstances described in the country report.

Mexico established a landmark precedent for the application of domestic FOIA when its Information Commission ordered the disclosure of documents related to a $108 million World Bank loan to the state of Guanajuato in 2005.[8] These successes create a rallying point for the active use of FOIAs in obtaining IFI-related information. FOIA compliance however needs to be strengthened.

3. Country case studies

Argentina[9]

Victor Ricco, Paula Granada and Angeles Pereira

Introduction

Access to information in Argentina is enshrined in various provisions of the National Constitution[10], Decree N° 1.172, which was passed by the National Executive Branch in 2003.

One of the annexes contained in the decree regulates access to information establishing the right of every person to access to information and provides a period of ten working days for the State to deliver such information. In addition, it provides for access to a justice mechanism in case of silence from the administration or denial to deliver the information requested. Finally, as regards the environment, this right is regulated under national Acts N° 25.675 and 25.831.

Argentina has not yet passed a law specifically recognising and regulating the right of access to public information at the national level, although there is a bill under discussion by the National Congress[11]. It is due to the lack of national regulation that at the local level certain provinces (such as the province of Cordoba) have enacted this right by themselves.

This has given rise to different provisions, terms and mechanisms for access to public information at the provincial level.

Throughout this research, the national decree provisions were used. For local projects financed by IFIs, legislation pertaining to Cordoba province, such as Act 8803 which contains similar provisions to the abovementioned national decree, was used.

The World Bank Group, the IABD, the IMF, the *Corporación Andina de Fomento* (CAF), the *Fondo para la Cuenca del Plata* and export credit agencies are the IFIs that are most active and finance most projects in Latin America, particularly in Argentina. Their impact is extremely relevant to the economic, political and social life of this country. At present, the World Bank is financing thirty-four projects amounting to a total of US$5,500 million devoted mainly to State reform and the execution of the most important political policies with direct impact on the citizens. Therefore, it is important that the IFIs play their role as funders but the projects that they sponsor throughout the region should be monitored.

Results

A total of twenty-four requests were submitted by CEDHA and the Institute for Educational Development and Social Action (IDEAS) to eight different bodies; three IFIs and five governmental bodies. The same requests that were submitted to the IFIs were also submitted to those governmental bodies implementing the projects financed by the IFI or that by virtue of their portfolio, could have information related to the respective IFI project. This was done in order to find out the degree of usefulness and efficiency of the existing domestic legislation in obtaining information related to the projects financed by IFIs.

The main results obtained from the information requests were as follows:

Result	IFIs	Argentina Government
Answered	4	2
Mute refusal	6	5
Unable to submit	2	3
Transferred	1	0
Refusal to accept	0	1
Total	13	11

Ultimately, only six requests resulted in disclosure; four from the IFIs and two from government, which only provided brief answers. Following is an analysis of the results from two perspectives: i) the results obtained according to the body to which the information was requested and ii) the results obtained according to the type of document requested.

Results according to institution:
World Bank Group[12]

A total of six requests were submitted to the World Bank Group. They responded to four requests. In the first two concerning minutes and summaries resulting from the meetings of the Board of Directors, the information was provided by email. One request related to an urban drainage project and a standard request to the IFC received a response by fax within three days of submitting the request, making reference to the World Bank's webpage. In addition, the World Bank office stated that the IFC did not prepare a country impact review for Argentina and it did not have country impact notes. None of the other project-related requests which were submitted a couple of weeks later received a response. The administration said that the person in charge of dealing with requests was on holiday and no one had been appointed in an acting capacity.

A meeting was held after the monitoring period with the official in charge of information. She explained about an international project of the Bank on access to information, which she had been spearheading in Argentina since February 2005 after having gone through 15 days of training. She said that there were plans to also open country offices in other countries to advance this project. She stated that she was in regular contact with the head of communications in Washington D.C who controls the project and there was a specialist librarian in the regional office in Argentina in charge of distributing information internally.

She demonstrated to us how to search for information on the InfoShop database, which contains all official information and documents. She also informed us about different projects that the Bank was working on, one of which includes a website which allows information searches to be conducted with an interactive geographic map or by topic. This project had begun in Argentina and would be replicated elsewhere. The website was not yet available to the public but was being used internally. At the end of the interview, she provided us with the requested documents in hard copy.

Inter American Development Bank (IADB)[13]

Three requests were submitted to the IADB; one for the Country Strategy Paper and two relating to the projects *'Apoyo a la Modernización del Estado de la Provincia de Cordoba'* and *'Mejoramiento de Barrios'*.

None of these requests were responded to after waiting for two months, despite follow-up phone calls and emails which went unanswered.

During an interview with the official in charge of the Access to Public Information Service in Washington D.C, we shared the project objectives and the results of the requests submitted to the local IADB office. The official responded saying *'...it is a shame that people in the countries of the region only get the image shown by the local representatives, and that they do not get to know their daily work on improving the access to public information from our section here in Washington. But we are to blame, and we are going to fix it...'* Subsequently, he committed to following up the matter and asked for a meeting with CEDHA at a later date.

In January 2006, long after the official monitoring period, he provided a response to two of the requests submitted in 2005, by emailing links to their website which contained the information publicly available on the projects. The request for the current Country Strategy Paper was never responded to.

Corporación Andina de Fomento (CAF)[14]

CEDHA submitted a specific request about the project *Belo Horizonte – Brazil/ Argentina Border group 1 of the Iniciativa de Integración Regional de Sudamericana* (IIrsa). The institution answered on time that the request was transferred to the Secretary of Public Investment Territorial Planning *(Planificación Territorial de la Inversion Pública)*. The Secretary of Public Investment Territorial Planning never responded.

National Government

Three requests were submitted to the national office of projects with international credit agencies *(Dirección Nacional de Proyectos con Organismos Internacionales de Créditos)* regarding a risk management paper and environmental impact assessment documents of the World Bank project number 88220. This is part of the Ministry of Economy which is the office that manages all the IFIs' projects and is divided into three areas: World Bank Projects, IADB Projects and other IFIs projects (where the CAF project is located).

Two requests for IMF documents were submitted to the Ministry of Economy. Requests were also sent to the National Women Council, and the Ministry of Labour, Employment and Human Resources.

9

None of these requests were answered. To elaborate further:

a) *National Office of Projects with International Credit Bodies of the Ministry of Economy (Dirección Nacional de Proyectos con Organismos Internacionales de Créditos del Ministerio de Economía):*

Five of the requests submitted fell into the category of mute refusal. In an informal interview with the Governmental Manager of the IADB, we got some answers regarding the silence of the three governmental agencies in charge of keeping up the relationship between the IFIs and Argentina. The main results from this interview led us to conclude that:

★ There is not an active relationship between the governmental office in charge of projects related to IFIs and civil society.

The official explained to us that: *'we do not usually have information requests and we do not really have time to answer those requests.'*

★ There are internal obstacles between the government and the IFIs that hinder access to public information.

In the same interview, the manager attributed the delay in responding to the requests to the project number assigned by the IFI's administration. He said that the number was changed when the government took up the loan and the project could not be identified because it was classified under a different number.

★ There is a need to develop access to information mechanisms related to IFI projects involving the government.

When asked about how to obtain the number of projects assigned by the Argentina government, he said that they did not have public access to that information. He also stated that he was keen on creating a website where people could access this information, but at the moment could only offer to send a list with the government project numbers. He asked us to send a request asking for this information. Such a request was made but no answer was received.

We also asked for the latest written statement presented to the Board from the Country Executive Director in a meeting where the current CAS was discussed, as well as the summary of the board meeting on World Bank Disclosure Policy: Additional Issues, November 18th, 2004. Copies of our requests were shown to us at the interview and the official said that they would respond by post but we did not receive any documents.

b) *International Monetary Fund Office of the Ministry of Economy:*

Attempts to request minutes of the debate that took place at the latest meeting of the IMF Executive Directors, the concluding statements of the most recent Article IV mission and a full schedule of the upcoming Article IV mission to Argentina proved futile. It was physically impossible to file the requests because we could neither find the headquarters of the institution in Argentina nor obtain the address. We also sent information requests to the Public Information Officer of the Ministry of Economy, who offered to verify the contact of the local office in charge of the relation with the IMF, but no answer was obtained.

Local Government

A request was submitted to the Pro Cordoba Agency related to the local project *'Modernización del Estado'*. Another was submitted to the Ministry of Solidarity of Cordoba asking for a copy of the general document concerning the local project *'Mejoramiento de Barrios'*. Neither of these requests were answered, instead the local government was mute.

Results according to type of document

Requests were submitted regarding three types of documents: a) documents related to domestic decisions within the IFIs, b) documents related to the structure and financing of regional and local projects, and c) documents related to the EIAs of the financed projects.

Documents related to domestic decisions within the IFIs

Summaries of the meetings of IFIs' directors were requested as well as documents related to CASs and Article IV missions of the IMF. Out of the documents received from the World Bank, only two were disclosed within the two-month monitoring period. The rest were disclosed during the interview which took place after the prescribed monitoring period and after the World Bank had been informed about the monitoring.

Thus, we found out that while the Bank has a number of projects oriented towards strengthening access to information, it has not yet succeeded in putting in place a mechanism that ensures public access and compliance with its own policy. Particularly, it is necessary to reinforce the points related to the time-frame in which the request shall be replied to and the quality of the information that shall be sent to the requester.

On the other hand, the government office in charge of maintaining the relationship and contact with the IFIs is the Office of International Credit Bodies. This office did not disclose any of the documents and indicated during the informal interview that this type of information was not available at any Argentina-based office but had to be requested from the office of the Argentine Representative in Washington D.C.

In our opinion, the omission or obstruction of these mechanisms could severely hinder compliance with the terms of access to information provided for by the Argentine law and in accordance with national regulations. The State only has ten working days to comply with its obligation to inform. It is worth noting though that the State could also make use of the exception to extend the period by ten additional days if it justifies this need and informs the requester in due time.

Documents related to the structure and financing of regional and local projects.

Copies of the original general documents were requested containing the objectives, activities, time-frames, agendas, and a list of sub-projects related to two regional Integration of South American Regional Infrastructure (IIRSA) projects: *Autopista 60 de Valparaíso- Ferrovía los Andes de Chile and Belo Horizonte- Brazil*, and two local projects: 'Mejoramiento de Barrios' and *'Reforma del Estado'*.

In the case of the project *Autopista 60 de Valparaíso- Ferrovía los Andes de Chile* sponsored by the IADB, the documents were provided late. In the case of the second regional project financed by CAF, the response came from the same person, on behalf of the government and the IFI simultaneously. This peculiarity is due to the fact that this IFI has a government-based official as its country representative. Therefore, all the requests submitted regarding CAF-supported projects fall in the hands of the same person. As it was not possible to meet with this person, it was also not possible to identify the nature of this dual relationship. It would have been particularly important to conduct this interview as the CAF is an institution that lacks any kind of policy or regulation regarding information disclosure, while the government has specific standards regulating such access, and the lack of compliance opens specific access to justice channels.

In our opinion, the office only complies with certain access to information standards provided for by national law, such as the one related to time-frame. However, there are a number of standards that get shoved aside, such as the information quality aspect, which according to National Decree 1172, must be complete and clear, while in our experience the answers were brief and lacking in detail.

Documents related to Environmental Impact Assessments (EIAs) of financed projects.

A total of eight information requests were submitted concerning the EIAs of four projects related to local development. None of these requests were answered by the IFIs or the government. In our opinion, the disclosure policies established by the IFIs as well as the ones pertaining to local legislation were clearly infringed.

Argentina: Conclusions and recommendations

❖ In our opinion, it is much more fruitful to request IFI information from government bodies due to the more detailed and regulated mechanisms to access justice upon the denial of a response, or silence to such requests. Likewise, national regulations in Argentina provide the citizen with a time-frame slightly shorter than the one established by the IFIs for responding to requests. Although in practice the State has not been diligent in replying, legal action can be taken to obtain such information, which is not possible when the IFI is the one not giving the information. In turn, government officials who do not provide such information fail to comply with their duty as public officials which in Argentina is a crime and can be criminally sanctioned, adding further pressure to achieve compliance with the law.

11

- The lack of knowledge on the part of officials from both sides – the government and the IFIs – on the obligations regarding the right to information that derive from the disclosure policies and the FOI-type legislation is evident. We strongly recommend solid training of officials handling access to information within the IFIs and government. This not only refers to the specific public information office and the reception desks but also to all people who are involved e.g. legal officers, project officers and secretaries, because it is within these phases that obstacles mostly arise.

◇ There is a clear need to achieve a better system for administering access to IFI-related information between the IFIs and the government, especially regarding compliance with time-frames and other procedural obligations.

- There is a weak relationship between the IFIs and the governmental agencies in charge of nurturing and sustaining the relationship between these institutions and civil society. More efforts should be devoted to strengthening communication channels and participation of civil society in projects being implemented with IFIs´ financing. These efforts should be reflected in facilitated access to public information, human resources capacity building and external actions to connect citizens with public institutions and publish the different access to information mechanisms.

- Generally, the answers to information requests provided by IFIs and the government are of a low quality. Information quality, which refers to complete, truthful, adequate and timely information, is fundamental for proper compliance with the obligations established under the national legislation and the policies that the IFIs impose in this respect. The replies do not meet minimum standards concerning access to information at the international level. As regards this specific issue, national legislation contains better specifications on the type and quality of information that the State must provide.

- Finally, some positive impacts from the monitoring project:

  a) Concerning IFIs: The IADB requested CEDHA's collaboration to work on a document intended to enhance and optimise compliance with its policy of information disclosure, in relation to time-frame and information quality. Currently, we are working together on the elaboration of a document that regulates such provisions. Similarly, the IADB office in charge of the Public Information Center *(Centro de Información Publica)* in Buenos Aires, as well as the section in charge of civil society relations has been in contact with civil society hoping to establish a more active exchange.

  b) Concerning the government: Several bodies, particularly at the local level in Cordoba Province, have expressed their wish to conduct capacity-building activities jointly with civil society groups in order to collaborate on matters of access to information.

Bulgaria[15]

Nikolay Marekov

Introduction

THE *CO-ORDINATED FREEDOM of Information Monitoring* project began in Bulgaria in May 2005 with a series of meetings between the AIP and CEE Bankwatch representatives For the Earth and the Centre for Environmental Education and Information. During the meetings we discussed the contents of the requests and the time-frame of the project.

The summer of 2005 was a politically dynamic one in Bulgaria. Parliamentary elections were followed by a two-month period of consultations and a new Cabinet was formed in August. AIP has been closely monitoring closely the work of Bulgarian institutions during the last few years.[16] This is why we feel that we are in a position to draw conclusions and comment on the outcomes of the filed requests.

The Access to Public Information Act (APIA), adopted in 2000, regulates access to public information in Bulgaria. It stipulates that every Bulgarian citizen, foreigner or person without citizenship, as well as every organisation, has the right to request and subsequently receive information.

The APIA brought in obligations for government institutions to publish the following kinds of information on their own initiative: information that is likely to prevent threats to the citizens' life, health or security, or to their property; information that could disprove incorrect information that has been previously released; and information that could be of interest to the public or that must be prepared and released by virtue of another law.

The adoption of the Protection of Classified Information Act (PCIA) and the Protection of Personal Data Act (PDPA) in 2002 completed the legal framework for exemptions to the right of access to public information. Unfortunately, the Bulgarian legislation does not provide for a balance between the right to information and its limitations in every case.

The World Bank, the EIB and the European Bank for Reconstruction and Development (EBRD) are the IFIs which provide most funding for projects in

Bulgaria. As of March 31, 2002, total World Bank lending to Bulgaria amounted to US$1.5431 billion for twenty-seven operations. These included nine adjustment operations (US$870.8 million) and eighteen investment loans (US$672.3 million).[17] Large infrastructural projects and environmental projects are financed by the Instrument for Structural Policies for Pre-Accession (ISPA) programme of the European Union.

In the past few years, some national institutions have been intensely criticised for failing to implement projects financed by IFIs and for having to return the funding. In the course of this study, the AIP and For the Earth mainly requested access to documents related to statements, opinions and other communication between the Bulgarian government and IFIs in relation to the implementation of projects financed by the IFIs.

Result	IFIs	Bulgarian institutions
Mute refusal	3	2
Refusal	3	-
Information received	6	4
Incomplete information	-	4
Information not held	1	1

The table above shows a few similarities and differences between Bulgarian governmental institutions and IFIs. Most notably, the number of mute refusals is the same. Only IFIs issued explicit refusals, while Bulgarian governmental institutions often provided us with incomplete information. In some cases, Bulgarian institutions insisted that they did not hold the requested information, which was clearly related to the implementation of externally financed projects.

Results by Institution: IFIs
World Bank

The World Bank office in Bulgaria promptly provided the information that we requested. A day after

13

the requests were received, the World Bank contact person telephoned to specify how he would send the requested information. When the information was contained in relatively small files, they were sent by email. Bigger files were copied to a CD and delivered to the office of For the Earth. The World Bank turned down only one of the requests, where we had requested the list of all documents (full correspondence) between the Bank and the Government of Bulgaria in relation to the Programme Adjustment Loans (PAL) programme.[18] It turned out that the compilation of such a list would be very time consuming, so we decided to withdraw the request.

The project team believes that as an important part of the information promotion measures, the World Bank should publish their information policy in local languages. This is why we requested a copy of the Information Policy in Bulgarian. The World Bank office in Sofia responded by saying that it was not available, despite the fact that Bulgaria was one of the pilot countries included in the Document Translation Framework for the World Bank Group and Strengthening Public Information Centres programme.[19]

European Investment Bank (EIB)

As expected, the EIB's responses came very slowly. The request for the official position of the EIB in relation to Financial Contract FI No 20.60 for the construction of Trakia Highway was filed by email on 2 June 2005 and the EIB acknowledged that they had received it eight days later. On 22 July 2005, we received an answer containing links to two press-releases expressing the position of the Bank concerning '...the construction of two sections covering a total of 75 km of the Orizovo-Burgas motorway, which is part of "Priority Corridor VIII" of the Pan-European Road Network for Central and Eastern Europe'. Three days later, we specified the request explaining that we would have liked to receive access to an official document (letter, sent to the Bulgarian government), expressing the position of the Bank on the project. On 10 August 2005, access to the document was refused, because 'this correspondence between the EIB and the Bulgarian Government falls within the normal confidential bank-customer relationship, which is covered in the Articles 4.1.vii and 4.3 of the EIB "Rules on Public Access to Documents", and therefore cannot be

released. However, should the Bulgarian Government decide to release such information to the public, the EIB would have no objections.'

The Ministry of Regional Development and Public Works never answered our request for access to this document and the EIB never asked for its consent. We are inclined to believe that the official document had been previously disclosed to a Bulgarian newspaper following their informal request.[20]

The other request filed to the EIB was the Letter of the EIB REF No. H4 (2005)A/1648 from 24/01/2005.[21] Exactly two months after filing the request, we received an email informing us that the response period would have to be extended. After waiting for a reply for an additional two months, we filed an official complaint with the Secretary General and General Counsel. In response, we received a reply explaining that our request had indeed been considered complex because the reference of the document was not an EIB reference number, but an internal letter sent to the European Commission referring to a project which was still under appraisal and involved documents to be provided by the promoter.

The EIB did not explain what an internal document sent to the European Commission was, nor did they provide any explanation why disclosing the document could possibly impede the implementation of the project. We have to note yet again here that the Bulgarian Ministry of Energy and Water simply ignored the identical request which concerned the construction of the National Hazardous Waste Centre near the town of Radnevo. For the Earth has been working on this case for a number of years and has collected some valuable information.[22] The project team believes that cases like this should be further explored and publicised with possible case studies and publications.

European Bank for Reconstruction and Development (EBRD)

The EBRD provided no response whatsoever to our information requests within the project period. It is not uncommon for the EBRD to provide information with significant delays and sometimes even to ignore information requests. In comparison, we received from the Ministry of Energy and Energy Resources information about the list of all projects funded or co-funded by the Kozloduy International De-comissioning Support Fund, administered by the EBRD.[23] We also received the concession contract between the Municipality of Sofia and International Water/United Utilities from the Council of Ministers.

International Monetary Fund (IMF)

The IMF office responded immediately and provided us with a weblink. The IMF does not often receive information requests, so they could spare the time to respond (which they did on the very same day that the request was submitted). The answer was quite brief and formal, instructing us to browse the web page of the IMF.

International Financial Corporation (IFC)

Only one request was filed to the IFC during the project period. The IFC assured us that the request had been received and would be handled. The request was later transferred to another department, but we never heard from them afterwards.

European Commission (EC)

As noted above, the project team decided to submit the request about the National Hazardous Waste Center (NHWC) in Radnevo to the European Commission. For technical reasons, a response was received after more than a month (a violation of Regulation 1049/2001). The request was forwarded to the EIB, because the requested documents '...[were] the documents of the European Investment Bank'. As mentioned earlier in this report, the request to the EIB was answered only after we filed an official complaint to the Secretary General and General Counsel.

Results by institution
Ministry of Finance

Due to its functions and activities, the Ministry of Finance has been subjected to a comparatively large number of FOI requests since the adoption of the Bulgarian APIA in 2000. An information official has been appointed by an order of the Minister and internal procedures for handling information requests have been adopted. Although this has some positive aspects such as clearly assigned responsibilities and easier contact with the information official, it also formalises the procedure and sometimes creates difficulties for the requesters. The Ministry of Finance provided complete information following three of the four requests but sometimes did so with considerable delay.

For example, the request for the Summary of Board Meetings on World Bank Disclosure Policy: Additional Issues, November 18, 2004 was responded to within a single day by email, while the Ministry asked for the consent of the World Bank and replied after six weeks (which was two weeks beyond the legally mandated period).

Another example was the request for IMF concluding statements and assessments following the Article IV consultations with Bulgaria in 2004. On the last day before the deadline, the Ministry replied with a request for clarification, insisting that Article IV consultations with Bulgaria had been held on a number of occasions in 2004. Only after contacting the information official by email and telephone stating that we preferred an email answer and had no intention of filing a complaint, did they provide a quick answer.

Conclusion: *The Ministry generally tries to comply with the law and its internal procedures. However, blindly following the procedures may sometimes lead to ineffective flow of information. Often, the Ministry uses vague reasoning to withhold information about internationally financed projects, that should normally be published on their website (like feasibility studies, financial memoranda, cost benefit analyses and application forms for ISPA projects).*[24]

Council of Ministers

The situation with the Council of Ministers is to a large extent similar to the one in the Ministry of Finance. An official from the Government Information Service (GIS) is responsible for handling information requests. Formally, all four requests filed to the GIS received an answer. However, none of the answers was as complete as we had wished. In the case of the three World Bank requests, for example, we were given links to the Bank's website. The office of the World Bank in Sofia on the other hand, responded with a couple of phone calls and a CD containing more accessible and well-organised information.

Ministry of Energy and Energy Resources

Only one request was filed to the Ministry during the project period. The request was answered

Problem: *Every time you hand-deliver a request to the GIS, you have to return the next day to receive a log number. Obviously, this procedure puts a burden on the requester.*

Conclusion: *The Council of Ministers is an institution which receives and handles a large number of information requests. As a result, they have established a procedure and have clear responsibilities assigned. Largely due to public scrutiny (including from media), the GIS cannot afford to ignore requests but the quality of the information provided is not always good.*

promptly and the information provided was complete. The Ministry has established clear procedures for information disclosure and published them online. Unfortunately in this respect, with the change of political power, this Ministry will become part of the Ministry of Economy. Our experience with the latter shows that formalities hinder efficient access to information.

Ministry of Regional Development and Public Works

The Ministry has some internal rules for document handling and information provision. However, there have been cases of mute refusals before. During the study, we filed one request[25] to them and received an answer that the information was not held. In comparison, following a similar request to the EIB, we initially received some general information. After clarifying the request, the EIB refused to provide us a copy of the document, stating that 'correspondence between the EIB and the Bulgarian Government fell within the normal confidential bank-customer relationship, which was covered in the Articles 4.1.vii and 4.3 of the EIB Rules on Public Access to Documents.'

Ministry of Environment and Water

The Minister has regulated the procedures of information provision with three orders and an information official has been authorised to handle requests. Despite this, we received no answer to the request we submitted.[26] One of the main functions of the Ministry of Environment and Water is to actively provide information about projects affecting the environment and to encourage citizens and affected groups to participate in the decision-making process. However, on numerous occasions the Ministry has refused to provide important information on grounds which warrant questions. Minutes of public discussions of EIA reports have been withheld with the explanation that they have no significance on their own. Application forms, feasibility studies and cost benefit analyses have been withheld because they are 'preliminary documents', while declarations of experts authorised to work on EIAs have been refused because they contain 'personal data'.

Municipality of Sofia

In 2000, Sofiyska Voda AD took over the operation of the water and wastewater services of Sofia through a 25-year concession agreement signed with the Municipality of Sofia. The project team decided to request information about the concession contract both from the Municipality and from the Council of Ministers.[27] The Municipality refused to provide a copy of the contract because consent of the third party (the concessioner) was required. No indications were given whether this consent had actually been requested. After a brief clarification, the Council of Ministers did provide us with a weblink to the server of the Municipality (http://www.sofia.bg/template4.asp?ime=KONCES %7D), where the contract (without the requested attachments) could be downloaded. However, this link cannot be reached by browsing the web site of the Municipality.

The Mayor of Sofia has been intensely criticised for failing to provide access to public information. In the 2005 Right to Know Day award ceremony[28] organised by AIP, the Municipality of Sofia received a *dishonorary diploma* for the total lack of information about measures taken to overcome the waste management crisis in Sofia in the summer of 2005.

Results by type of documents

The project team requested three main kinds of documents: project-related documentation (contracts and reports), consultation documents (statements, opinions and other correspondence between the Bulgarian government and IFIs) and assessment reports and final documents of the IFIs. We also decided to file a request for the World Bank information disclosure policy in Bulgarian. What we believed would be a routine request resulted in non-disclosure because a Bulgarian translation of the policy was unavailable.

Project-related documents

The project team requested: the matrices and implementation reports of all PAL projects for Bulgaria (from the World Bank and the Council of Ministers); the concession contract between the Municipality of Sofia and International Water/ United Utilities; a list of all projects funded or co-funded by the Kozloduy International Decomissioning Support Fund administered by the EBRD; and a list of approved IFC projects for Bulgaria.

With the exception of the last request, we received some kind of information from at least one institution. The World Bank answered completely and immediately, as did the Ministry of Energy and Energy Resources. The EBRD did not give an answer to any of the requests although they had published some information on their website.

Consultation documents

Written statements of the World Bank or the EBRD, letters of the EIB with regard to the implementation of a project and written statements of the Bulgarian government before the World Bank were requested. Only one request resulted in complete disclosure – the latest written statement presented to the World Bank from the Country Executive Director on CAS. In all the remaining cases, the outcomes were unsatisfactory – two mute refusals, three explicit refusals, an incomplete answer and an answer of 'information not held'. Most notably the EIB turned down two requests, because the information fell within confidential bank-customer relationships. It was therefore difficult to access correspondence between the IFIs and local government.

IFI's assessment reports and final documents

We requested Summary of Board Meetings on World Bank Disclosure Policy: Additional Issues, November 18, 2004, the IMF report adopted in 2004 covering long-term relationships between the Fund and Bulgaria and the IMF concluding statements and assessments following the Article IV consultations with Bulgaria in 2004.

All requests were answered promptly and in full. Both IFIs and national government institutions provided information electronically (by email or an Internet address).

Bulgaria: Conclusions and recommendations

Specific problems and their relation to the GTI IFI Transparency Charter principles[29] are presented below:

- The European Commission and the EIB refused to provide access to documents arguing that they had not created them.[30] This violates Principle 1 of the GTI Transparency Charter, which states that: '...The right [of access to information] applies to all information held by an IFI, regardless of who produced it.'

- In a number of cases, especially where we requested a list of documents, project-related or other correspondence, we received weblinks in response (e.g. the request filed to the IMF, or the Council of Ministers). This contradicts Principle 2: '..Where a request is accepted, access should be given in the form requested...This should include, as necessary, extracting relevant information from databases and reasonable processing/collating of such information to provide it in a form which is accessible for the requester.'

- The procedure for filing requests and obtaining log numbers from the Council of Ministers should be changed, because it burdens the requesters. In view of the importance of the Cabinet activities, we would recommend that the GIS accept requests in different forms. The Bulgarian Ministry of Finance and some of the IFIs provided information after email requests.

- Almost none of the requested documents were available in Bulgarian, even when we requested them from national institutions. Feasibility studies, application forms, cost benefit analyses and other project documentation are not available in Bulgarian from the Ministry of Finance or the Ministry of Environment and Water. This violates Principle 2 of the Charter: 'Where reasonably possible, information should be provided in the language requested and translation should always be provided where this is in the public interest, for example because the information is of interest to a whole community'. Furthermore, the information policy of the World Bank was not available in Bulgarian even at the Bank's office in Bulgaria.

- In many cases, national authorities withheld information about internationally financed

17

projects, explaining that they did not have the consent of the financing institutions.[31] We would expect such documents to be published routinely by the Ministry because they concern projects of great public interest. We consider this also a violation of Principle 3 of the Charter, which states that 'IFIs should routinely disclose a wide range of information about their structure, policies and prodecures, decision-making processes and country and project work in a timely fashion'.

◆ The refusal of the IFIs to provide information violated Principle 4 of the Charter: 'Access to particular information should be refused only where the IFI demonstrates, on a case-by-case basis at the time of the request, that disclosure would cause serious harm to one of the interests listed and that this harm outweighs the public interest in accessing the information'. In both

refusals the EIB referred to its information policy, but failed to demonstrate how the disclosure of the requested document was likely to harm a specific interest.

◆ Only one complaint was filed by the project team to an IFI (the EIB). The EIB only accepts complaints sent by regular mail, which slows the process considerably. IFIs should comply with Principle 7 of the Charter: '...it should be possible to lodge a complaint in a number of ways, including by fax, email or regular mail...'

◆ As seen from their response, the EIB obviously had problems identifying one of the requested documents – a letter sent to the European Commission. This is not in compliance with Principle 8 of the Charter: '...Putting in place an effective and progressive system of records management...'

Mexico[32]

Issa Luna Pla

Introduction

This report presents the results of an empirical requesting exercise conducted in Mexico in 2005 where requests were submitted to three IFIs and three government ministries. The requests were made in line with IFI information disclosure policies and the Federal Transparency and Access to Public Government Information Law.

Results by institution

The IFIs that are most active in Mexico are the World Bank Group, the IADB and the IMF.

International Monetary Fund (IMF)

All information was requested by email and no answer whatsoever was received in the three attempts made by the requester. All four requests were submitted by email to the General Enquiries and the NGO Relationship Office email addresses in English and in Spanish. Phone interviews were requested without any response. The IMF therefore ignored all sorts of communication from LIMAC.

World Bank Group

None of the documents requested from the World Bank office in Mexico City was disclosed. However, refusals were given, mostly grounded in paragraph 86 of the World Bank Policy on Disclosure of Information, 2002.[33] Regarding the request for Country Impact Review and Country Impact Notes, the World Bank Mexican office responded by saying the documents were unknown to them.

Overall, the requester perceived a good attitude in the World Bank office. Requests were responded to within ten days and in cases were the Public Information Centre (PIC) needed more time, the requester was informed of this ahead of time. There was good communication between the PIC in Mexico and the requestor and each request was responded to individually. In cases where the request was not clear, clarification was sought from the requester.

Where the requested information was considered classified, reasons grounded in the disclosure policy were given.

During the interview with the Public Information Assistant at the World Bank PIC, the official expressed surprise on hearing that the requests were part of a larger monitoring exercise but was very responsive to discussing the internal procedures for handling requests and willing to resolve any issues arising from the requests.

According to the official, once they receive a request, they make an effort to contact requesters to better understand their inquiries and meet their expectations although this is not required by the information disclosure policy. Once a request is received, internal consultations are held with the department that could hold the information. In some cases this could be the Bank archives in Washington D.C.

The interpretation of the World Bank Disclosure Policy is not subjective; the list of disclosed documents is clear and there is no room for interpretation. PIC officers just have to follow the policy literally. In the case of doubt, the PIC consults with the head office in Washington D.C. to confirm the status of classified documents. Even though the World Bank Disclosure Policy does not establish any appeal process to review refusals of information, the PIC welcomes complaints but there is no possibility of reversing the outcome if it is a direct interpretation of the policy.

In addition to facilitating access to information, the PIC promotes the Bank's activities through fairs, conferences and other public events. According to the official, there is a shared feeling in the Bank that NGOs see the Bank as a 'monster that dictates policies to governments in countries', and therefore demand more information from the Bank.

PIC staff have been trained on the functioning of the World Bank Group institutions and on their responsibilities in implementing the disclosure policy. World Bank PICs around the world work together closely to better implement the disclosure policy.

Inter American Development Bank (IADB)

Three requests were submitted to the IADB office in Mexico City. Two resulted in incomplete answers and no information was held on the third request. Some of the main problems in trying to get information from the IADB are outlined below:

◆ The requester asked twice for the Country Strategy Paper and instead, the IADB information centre sent the website link to the CAS.

◆ The requester asked for a copy of original documents produced during the data collection for the Information, Consultation and Participation (ICP) Initiative applied in Mexico for the Plan Puebla Panama prior to restructuring. The IADB office referred to the general Plan Puebla Panama link, which contained no such information.

◆ The requester asked for the reports and ex post evaluations of the finalised projects in the last 10 years in Mexico. The IADB office avoided the question until a face-to-face interview was held, in which the officer argued that there had been no reports to date.

The requester had to send the information requests three times before getting a response from the PIC. The attitude was therefore perceived by the requester as negative and uncaring. The requester was frustrated because the contact person kept trying to evade the questions by giving the wrong information instead of outrightly providing an official negative response. The Information Disclosure Policy was not referred to as legal grounds for denying any information; instead the official chose to withhold the information by sending unrelated documents.

An interview with the librarian and expert on information systems, who heads the PIC at the IADB office shed light on how the PIC works and how requests for information are dealt with. The official was surprised to hear that he was the subject of a testing exercise by the GTI and was uncomfortable about not having been told in advance. Although he was open, he offered unspecific responses to the questions posed to him.

He explained that the PIC receives requests submitted by different means and that most of them are questions about where to find information on the IADB's website. The information available in the PIC, which resembles a small library, and the information posted on the website are the only information sources for answering requests. This means that no internal consultations are held with other departments and no other sources are referred to in facilitating access to information to the public.

The PIC, which comprises two staff, deals with the media, and functions as a library and a bookshop. On average, the PIC receives about 15 requests ranging from contact information of staff to more substantial requests for internal documents. The requesters are mainly academics, the Central Bank of Mexico and international organisations. Requests are responded to as soon as possible mostly by internet with links to the website. Usually, an effort is made to send documents by post when the requester lives outside Mexico City. The centre generates statistics regarding the number of requests and their outcomes but those are not publicly available.

The official acknowledged that the IADB disclosure policy is not well understood by the internal staff adding that employees sign confidentiality contracts when hired by the Bank. The 2003 disclosure policy was presented to the staff in Mexico and discussed internally but no training on the implementation and interpretation of the policy was given to the PIC staff. There is also little awareness of the federal access to information law in Mexico, which is relatively recent and its use still undeveloped. The Bank is currently focussing on disseminating more information on its activities through an outreach campaign.

The PIC has an unwritten policy to never refuse information to requesters, because it is 'inappropriate' to deny information. In cases where certain information requested is considered classified, the PIC gives the requester other information which it considers to be either related to the request or of interest to the requester.

Mexican ministries

All the requests made to Mexican ministries were answered in a timely manner according to the Federal Transparency and Access to Public Government Information Law (LFTAIP). The Ministry of Exterior Affairs (*Secretaria de Relaciones Exteriores*) and the President's Office referred all the requests either to the IFIs offices or to other ministries. The Ministry of Finance also referred most of the requests, the difference being that the liaison office gave very accurate indications of where to find the information (or related data) in the IMF and World Bank's websites. These referrals were related to the requests for the World Bank Summary of Directory Board Meetings on the Disclosure Policy: Additional Issues from November 18, 2004; World Bank reports on finalised projects in Mexico; and Minutes of discussion at the latest meeting of the Executive Directors of the IMF. The Ministry of Finance also referred questions to one local government as a beneficiary of the *Decentralized Infrastructure Reform and Development Loan Project*, in which the National Bank of Public Works and Services (Banobras) is acting as financial agent for the state of Guanajuato.

There were two cases where information was disclosed by the Ministry of Finance. The documents on the project *'Equidad de Genero'* loan number 7022-ME implemented by the Women National Institute, were provided electronically via the internet. In addition, the liaison office provided the exact weblink in the Ministry's website where the concluding statement from the most recent Article IV Mission of the IMF was located, published in the IMF website in 2005. These two answers were to the full satisfaction of the requester.

The Ministry of Finance delivered an incomplete answer to the request for the latest written statement presented to the Board from the Country Executive Director on the meeting where the present CAS was discussed of the World Bank. In this case, instead of disclosing the written statement, the CAS was provided, without the documents of the decision process as requested.

The government liaison staff were formal and acted in compliance with the procedures entrenched in the legal framework. This means that they asked the requester for clarification on the requests when in doubt, responded within the ten working days deadline and consulted with the internal committee before issuing a response.

Results by type of documents
Minutes or summaries of meeting
The World Bank refused to disclose board meeting minutes arguing that they only became publicly available from April 1, 2005 and that the policy did not apply retroactively. Related questions were denied under paragraph 83 of the disclosure policy.

Country Assistance Strategies (CASs)
These documents were either available on the IFIs' websites or were promptly sent to the requester. Mexican government offices are often familiar with the CAS and therefore quick to provide it.

Loan Contracts
The response to a request related to the awarding of loans was classified as information not held. This is because the World Bank said that it did not hold the information because the requested information was within the scope of the Mexican government. The requester asked for the minutes and documents related to the decision-making process for choosing the state of Guanajuato as eligible for a US$108.00 million loan. The World Bank PIC argued that the 'owner of the project', in this case the Mexican government, was responsible for the selection of the states, therefore the responsibility to hold and disclose the documents backing such a decision was in the Mexican government's realm.

Mexico: Conclusions and recommendations
- The IFI information disclosure policies do not have sufficient legal force to promote an enforceable right to access to information. In this regard, disclosure policies are seen as corporate governance guidelines with the weaker force of an ethical code.
- The IFIs treat all requests for information equally and their understanding of a request for information is anything from a request for contact details, a request inviting IFI staff to official meetings and events, to a request for specific documents or general information about the functioning of the IFI. Disclosure policies should make a clear distinction between the categories of public inquiries ranging from general to specific, which would necessitate the relevant processing avenues inside the institution.
- Staff of the IFIs are generally trained to deal with media and the press in a proactive way. This means that they are well prepared to distribute information about what the IFIs want

and decide to make public. However, the IFIs are unwilling to disclose information that would expose project and management inefficiencies. This obstructs the adoption of more proactive disclosure policies. Staff should additionally be trained to interpret the disclosure policies and respond to information requests in the most appropriate manner.

◆ The IFI disclosure policies do not have the same high standards that the Mexican FOIA has, which grants greater access to information with clear procedures and recourse mechanisms.

◆ The Mexican Federal Government does not have a clear and pre-established record management policy on documents generated from affairs and business with IFIs. Hence, the Mexican government offices opt to refer

information requests to the IFIs rather than treat them under the national transparency and access to information law. As a consequence of the undefined legal responsibility to records management, minutes, open meetings and other information on deliberation processes are not disclosed to requesters.

◆ Appeals against refusals in the Mexican legal frame are only applicable to information held by the national government. This mechanism is useful in obtaining documents related to loan projects assigned to Mexican organisations. Nevertheless, appeal mechanisms within the IFIs themselves fall far short of the Mexican governmental FOIA standard, as well as the GTI Charter principles.

Slovakia[34]

Peter Mihok

Introduction

According to some observers, Slovakia has one of the strictest FOIAs in the world. Past experience of Friends of the Earth-CEPA showed that it is much easier to get IFI documents via relevant Slovak authorities that hold them than through IFIs. Not only is the response deadline within the Slovak FOIA short (at the time of submitting the requests, it was ten calendar days, with a legal option to increase it to 20 days should the request for information be difficult to process) but the Act also clearly spells out that every document which is not confidential under the FOIA or any other law must be released.

Some IFIs, in particular the EIB, had a tendency in the past to shift responsibility for releasing documents to the Slovak authorities. Typically the phrase 'the EIB has no objection should the promoter decide to disclose the information' was added to the text justifying the refusal to disclose the requested information.

This practice continued with requests sent to the EIB within the scope of this project. The World Bank, for example, found out by itself that we, through the mirror request we had sent to the government, had already received the requested information from the Slovak authorities and in its response only referred to this fact.

The GTI Co-ordinated Freedom of Information Monitoring project was realised within the planned time-frame. As Friends of the Earth-CEPA was already well known in the media as an organisation that sends out court appeals in cases where Slovak institutions violated the Slovak FOIA, a local and not well-known organisation, Uplift ('Vzpruha' in Slovak), was chosen as the partner organisation which submitted all the requests for project-related information.

In this report the outcomes of the testing are revealed and analysed. The first part, which sorts the results by type of institution, presents how all the tested institutions responded to requests for information and whether, in our opinion, they respected their own Public Information Disclosure policies and the Slovak FOIA respectively. The second part describes the type of documents requested and the results of these. The final section provides a conclusion and recommendations.

Results by the institutions: IFIs
International Monetary Fund (IMF)

Both standardised requests were answered together in one short informal email within three days. Regarding the date for the next Article IV mission to Slovakia, we only received preliminary information stating 'the date is not yet fixed ... it will probably be toward the end of 2005'. The IMF staff did not provide us with any other information, such as when the date would be decided and how the IMF would inform the public about this. Refusal to disclose minutes of a meeting was explained only with the phrase 'we don't share the minutes of meetings' without a reference to any official policy. Compare this response to the same request submitted to the Ministry of Finance later in the report.

We are of the opinion that the IMF answered our requests minimally, without any effort to help us execute our right to information and right to know the legal reasons for refusals.

International Bank for Reconstruction and Development (IBRD)

All four requests were sent to the local office and answered within approximately seven weeks, i.e. shortly before our two-month deadline. However, the Bank staff explained to us that the delay was caused by 'intensive travel'. Refusals to both standardised requests were well justified with clear reference to the information disclosure policy. Moreover, we were provided with a link to the Bank's webpage where the text of the policy is available. Thanks to the long-term good informal relationship between the Bank and Friends of the Earth–CEPA, there was intensive follow-up, both by email and in person.

Project-related requests were partially refused as the Bank could not disclose Aide Memoire documents due to their internal character, but the Bank staff provided us with sufficient information on legal possibilities to get these documents through a specific procedure, which first needs approval of the Government, and the Bank staff additionally offered to support us should we decide to initiate the procedure. The procedure had not yet been initiated by the time of writing this report because we were searching for an organisation focussed on the issue that would be interested in reading the relevant Aide Memoires.

The other project documents (loan contracts) were disclosed to us by the implementing agencies even before the Bank's involvement and the Bank's staff referred to this fact saying that we could get back to them if this was not the case.

We are of the opinion that the Bank staff handled our request properly, with honest effort to help us to execute our right to know. The Bank's information policy was at the time of our request being reviewed in Washington D.C. with internal video conferences for the Bank's staff to follow curtailing our efforts to secure an interview.

International Finance Corporation (IFC)

With the aim of testing the capacity of the regional office in Moscow to deal with requests for information, we decided to send one request by registered mail and the other by email. The first one ended up with a mute refusal. The second one was transferred to the headquarters but to the wrong department, which subsequently transferred it to another department that never got back to us, even after we sent them a reminder.

Even though we were notified by email on the routing of our request within the different departments of the IFC, the request ended up with a mute refusal, and with an 'out of office auto-reply' being sent to us after our reminder.

We are of the opinion that the IFC regional office in Moscow was completely unable to handle the requests properly and we are hoping that the implementation of the Bank's new information policy currently under review will attempt to solve this problem.

European Bank for Reconstruction and Development (EBRD)

Three requests were sent to the NGO liaison office at the Bank's headquarters in London. One of them asking for the current Bank strategy for Slovakia was answered within a week with all information we wanted provided to us over email. The two other requests were answered on the very last day of the two-month deadline. There was some controversy related to a project-related request, which is analysed in more detail in the following section on EIA documents.

We are of the opinion that the EBRD keeps up with its information policy, mostly due to the fact that the NGO liaison office checks whether the requests are being answered by the deadline. However, we think that more efforts could be made by the project departments to help citizens execute their right to know about the projects which affect them in detail.

European Investment Bank (EIB)

Two project-related requests were sent to the EIB. In the case where we asked for a copy of the loan contract, the EIB refused to disclose it to us, grounding the resolution in the Bank's information policy, however we consider it a misinterpretation of the policy.

The EIB information policy is currently under review so we did not appeal the decision. We appealed a very similar decision in the past without success and are currently working on an appeal to the European Ombudsman. In the case where we asked for a copy of the non-technical results of the EIA, we were not provided with an official document but with a leaflet and a link to the webpage of the project's investor which both contained the information we were looking for, so we considered it a partial success.

We are of the opinion that the EIB information policy is below the standards of the other IFIs. The policy is currently under review and we are hoping for positive measures to be adopted to better reflect the presumption of disclosure and combat misinterpretation of the policy by the Bank's staff.

Results by Slovak Ministries

Eleven requests were sent to four different ministries: six to the Ministry of Finance, three to the Ministry of Environment, one to the Ministry of

Health and one to the Ministry of Labour, Social Issues and Family.

All requests were answered within the ten-day deadline as set by the Slovak FOIA. There was only one controversial case when the document we wanted was not held by a Ministry and we were only informed of that informally by email i.e. the Ministry did not send us a response in the form of a legal resolution as is required. When we discussed this problem with them in person, we found out that different Ministries interpret the FOIA on this point differently, with the Ministry of Environment insisting that 'when the information is not available to us there is nothing to issue a legal decision about'.

The Ministry of Finance, which received most of the requests, strictly adhered to the Slovak FOIA. All responses in cases where IFI documents were not held by the Ministry were answered in the form of a legal decision, which would enable us to take legal action should we be convinced that the IFI documents we wanted could be unlawfully denied by the Ministries. In the case when the Ministry refused to disclose the IMF document, we were provided with a paper copy of the IMF's Founding Agreement Article IX Section 5, which served as a legal basis for the negative decision.

We are of the opinion that in terms of the Slovak FOIA, adding this section of IMF policy sufficiently served as a justification that the IMF as the creator of the document had objections to the release of this document by Slovak institutions holding it. Another example of proper execution of 'presumption of disclosure' is the fact that the Ministry of Finance discloses draft loan contracts with the EIB for public projects on its webpage on a regular basis.[35]

Within this project, we requested one loan contract with the EIB from the Ministry. In our request we referred to the version of the contract disclosed on the website of the Ministry and asked them to confirm that the disclosed copy was the final version signed with the EIB. In a short time, via email, we received a formal letter from them confirming that the text of the draft loan agreement which was posted on the website had not been modified in the final document. This mechanism proved that the access to updated information can happen rapidly, without the need for time-consuming paperwork at the Ministry.

Results by types of documents: IFIs
Minutes or summaries of meetings

None of the IFIs disclosed these types of documents to us. With the exception of the minutes of discussion from the meeting of the IMF Executive Directors on results of Article IV consultations with the Slovak Republic, none of the requested documents were held by the Ministry of Finance or other Slovak institution.

Country Assistance Strategies (CAS)

This type of document was available on the webpages of the EBRD and the IBRD. The EBRD also sent it to us as an email attachment within a few days of receiving the request. Our requests for information on the possibilities of NGOs participating in the process of creating these documents were handled sufficiently by both IFIs but we found out that Slovak Ministries were not kept up to date about the status of these processes and therefore could not provide sufficient information to us on how NGOs could take part in CAS processes.

Loan contracts

We requested loan contracts from the World Bank and the EIB. In the case of the World Bank, the loan agreements were disclosed to us by the implementing Government Ministries even before the Bank's approval was granted to the Ministries, due to the strict deadline for responding to requests set by the Slovak FOIA. The loan agreement for the Health Sector Modernisation Support Technical Assistance Project was disclosed on the internet webpage of the Office of the Slovak Government in 2003 and the Ministry of Health sent us a weblink where we could find the loan agreement. For the Social Benefits Reform Administration Project, a hard copy of the agreement in English was posted to us. The World Bank staff replied that the copies of loan contracts we requested from them had already been disclosed to us by the relevant Ministries mentioned above.

The EIB refused to provide us with a copy of a loan contract for a highway project. We consider this decision very controversial because this loan contract is publicly available on the internet webpage of the Ministry of Finance and the Office of the Slovak Government. As mentioned above, the Ministry of Finance responded to us in writing that the disclosed version was the final version signed with the EIB and was never modified. In the past, we appealed a similar decision of the EIB with no success. Within the scope of this project no appeal was lodged as the EIB Information Policy was under review.[36]

Environmental Impact Assessment (EIA) documents

We chose three projects to test disclosure of EIA documents. Two requests were related to the historical legal grounds under which these EIAs were prepared. In one case the EIA was done upon the IFI's request, even though this was not required under Slovak law. The other case was the opposite; the full EIA was requested by Slovak law but was not an required under the IFI's environmental policy. The third was an IFC project.

As a result of our requests, we found out that the IFIs did not exchange EIA documents with the relevant Slovak authorities and vice-versa. In the case of the EIB project where the EIA was a request of the Bank, the Ministry of Environment informed us that they did not have the EIA results available. This was despite the fact that we found out from the EIB that results of EIAs are publicly available on the webpage of the project promoter.

In the case of the EBRD, the full EIA was done because it was required by the Slovak EIA Act. Yet, the EBRD informed us that 'it is a B level project and therefore it does not require an EIA'. However, the EBRD provided the Project Summary Document by email which included some detailed information on the results of EIA for this project. Moreover, the statement we got from the EBRD contravenes the Bank's own environmental policy, which states that limited EIAs are required for category B projects. It therefore can be concluded that the EBRD project department tended to provide incorrect information rather than trying to help affected citizens find out information about the environmental impacts of Bank-supported projects through implementing agencies in the country.

In the case of the IFC project, the request resulted in a mute refusal and the request to the Ministry of Environment was transferred to the national office of the UN due to the fact that it was a Global Environment Facility (GEF) project. However, the UN could not identify the project because it had a different database of projects from the IFC. Furthermore, even after we provided the UN office with more information on which project EIA we had requested, referring to the IFC webpage, we ended up with a mute refusal.

Slovakia: General conclusions and recommendations

This project again proved our past general experience with requesting information from the IFIs, in particular that:

◆ When asking IFIs for information which is available on their websites, for example a CAS, they often answer within a few days, unlike when requesting project-related information.

◆ IFIs tend to answer on the last days of the generous deadlines granted to them by their own disclosure policies.

◆ The World Bank, the EBRD and the EIB deal with information requests formally; the IMF and the IFC respond in a very informal or otherwise limited way.

◆ IFIs generally prefer that their clients (project promoters, implementing agencies, etc) disclose project-related documents and information.

New information emerged through this project:

◆ The World Bank staff was willing to assist our partner NGO, Uplift, to initiate the procedure with the Slovak Government for releasing Aide Memoire documents for projects which are regarded as controversial in the media.

◆ There is lack of communication between IFIs and the relevant Slovak authorities. The Ministry of Finance did not have the minutes of meetings, the statements of foreign officials representing Slovakia in IFI governing bodies or information on possibilities for NGOs to participate in the CAS preparation processes. The EIB did not provide the Ministry of Environment with the EIA it had conducted for one of its projects.

◆ Mute refusals to requests submitted to the IFC and Slovak authorities, together with insufficient information on the IFC and GEF activities were received.

There were no problems with the execution of the FOIA by Slovak authorities, with the exception of one minor controversy where we were told informally that the requested document was not held by the public body.

IFIs often claim that execution of high information policy standards requested by NGOs, such as short response time-frames, presumption of disclosure, necessity to ground refusals on legal grounds, among others, would require a lot of new staff to be hired. Our experience with the Ministry of Finance suggests that this is not true and proves that when there is a will to be transparent, even a few people can fulfil all the high standards requested by NGOs. Our findings from the Ministry of Finance summarised below, where the Information Department consists of five members of staff, including the director and webmaster, show that these principles are, in our opinion, fully implementable by the IFIs. They include:

◈ **Presumption of disclosure:** This is clearly spelled out in the Slovak FOIA for documents which are created by the Slovak institutions but is also applied for documents such as loan agreements with IFIs even though the EIB considers loan contracts confidential and refuses to disclose them. The legal analysis done by the Ministry of Finance did not find the loan agreement to be sufficiently grounded in law and therefore fully respected the presumption of disclosure principle.

◈ **Timely disclosure:** The loan contracts with the EIB are disclosed by the Ministry of Finance several weeks before they are approved and signed by the Bank, giving the public an official right to comment on the content. This is also legally grounded in the Slovak legislation.

◈ **Competence of staff to complement each other:** Even a webmaster can handle incoming requests and transfer them to the appropriate department. This was implemented when there were a lot of incoming requests at the same time, for example.

◈ **Strict internal norms:** The internal policy and norms of the Ministry of Finance Information

Department require staff to forward requests for information to the appropriate department within one working day.

◈ **Grounding refusals in legal grounds:** This is an official obligation from the Information Department to all other departments; if they propose not to disclose the information they hold, they must provide the Information Department with a legal reason which justifies non-disclosure.

◈ **Pro-active disclosure of all frequently requested information:** The staff of all departments not only have the right to propose pro-active disclosure of certain types of documents, but the Act requires that the Minister is informed if some types of information are repeatedly requested, in which case this kind of information must henceforth be disclosed pro-actively and posted on the internet webpage after approval by the Minister.

◈ **Accommodating the needs and abilities of the public:** The Ministry, for example, after the restructuring of its webpage, still keeps its old webpage running to accommodate the needs of those who were used to it and wish to search for older information.

◈ **Positive approach to problem solving and willingness to comply:** Although there is a strict internal policy, the system of work is being managed continuously. The most important is the fact that the Ministry of Finance and its key staff consider transparency a crucial aspect not just of citizens' right to know, but also of their own protection and strive to work free of corruption and conflict of interest.

South Africa[37]

Catherine Musuva

Introduction

THE SOUTH AFRICAN PROMOTION of Access to Information Act PAIA of 2000 is widely viewed as an excellent piece of legislation in terms of its scope, despite the 30-day response period, which is relatively long compared to other international FOIA legislation. It not only covers information held by private bodies but also emphasises the right to information as a leverage right which is required for the exercise or protection of other rights.[38] Refusal by omission or mute refusals, where no formal reasons for withholding the information are ever communicated to the requester, continue to be a striking outcome of requests submitted to national government institutions. These have been the findings of the GTI Coordinated FOI Requesting project as well as those of previous diagnostic studies conducted on the implementation of PAIA in South Africa.[39] In spite of this, two cases where vital World Bank-related documents were disclosed using the domestic law and denied by the IFI are highlighted later in this chapter. Appeals were not lodged in the pilot study but will form part of any subsequent phases. The study identified four main obstacles to obtaining information: the centralisation of decision-making in the IFIs regarding requests for information; the problem of persistent mute refusals which points to weaknesses in compliance and gaps in PAIA and IFI disclosure policies; the lack of sanctions for non-compliance; and attitudes of officials towards promoting the right to know.

Results

Below are the summarised results of the information requests submitted to different IFIs and national government institutions:

Results by type of institution: IFIs

In order to investigate the extent to which domestic legislation can be used to obtain IFI-related information, the same requests which were submitted to

Outcome	IFI	Gov	Total
Information Received	2	3	5
Incomplete Answer	2	0	2
Refusal	3	1	4
Mute Refusal	6	7	13
Total	13	11	24

IFIs were also submitted to the following public bodies which are either implementing projects with IFIs or expected to hold key IFI information.

The World Bank (International Bank for Reconstruction and Development)

The World Bank has local offices and PICs in many member countries which are headed by staff with high academic qualifications. The local World Bank office responded swiftly to the first batch of requests for policy discussions citing a clause in the disclosure policy and another document which denied the disclosure of these documents.[40] Therefore, they acted in line with their policy.

During the interview, the World Bank staff maintained they did not receive the second batch of requests which were for Aide Memoires but added that even if the requests were re-submitted, they would have resulted in a refusal because Aide Memoirs cannot be disclosed according to their policy. The outcomes of these requests, which were sent by fax and email, were categorised as mute refusals.

The effectiveness of the local PIC in promoting transparency and accountability of the Bank's operations is stifled by the limited scope of the disclosure policy which denies access to key information under clauses in their policy, despite the fact that the information was available from the Ministry of Finance. Nevertheless, the staff of the World Bank dealt with the requests promptly and professionally. The interview involved an official from the local office and an official from the headquarters and they referred us to Bank staff in the headquarters that were more familiar with the information disclosure policy for further questions.

The International Finance Corporation (IFC)

It was unclear from the outset where the IFC request was to be submitted and a phone call was necessary to clarify this. The staff of the IFC who responded to the request sent a weblink to the World Bank website stating that the request should have been sent to the World Bank. She added that all publicly available information could be found by visiting the link she had provided. This brief and unhelpful response led the requester to ask for a hard copy of the documents, which the official said was not available because the Country Impact Review and Country Impact Notes for South Africa were between 200 and 400 pages long. When asked whether they could provide the documents at a fee to cover printing and mailing costs, the staff said that they did not charge any fee and she had already directed us to the information. The response did not promote the spirit of the right to know and the staff did not make any effort to assist the requester. Moreover, the link provided was that of a World Bank website which lists all publicly available documents during the project cycle. The requested documents were not listed in the way they had been articulated in the request and it was not clear whether these documents were not publicly available or whether such documents did not exist.

A letter was later sent to the IFC requesting a meeting to discuss the request and explain the project. The letter was addressed to the staff member who had responded to the request, because it was not clear to whom requests should be addressed. She came back saying that in fact she was not responsible for dealing with requests for information. We then requested that she transfer the letter to the relevant office. The letter did the rounds internally, finally ending up in the World Bank headquarters with the same official we had interviewed about the World Bank's policies and procedures who referred it yet again. No response to the request for a meeting was ever received.

We deduced that there was no person locally responsible for dealing with requests and that staff were uncertain about whether requests should be handled under the IFC disclosure policy or whether they fall under the World Bank's information disclo-

sure policy. In fact, there does not seem to be a structure for handling requests for information. The conduct of the IFC was unsatisfactory from a right to know perspective.

The International Monetary Fund (IMF)

The IMF does not have a local office and the requests were processed outside the country. It was not possible to identify the office bearers to whom requests should be addressed from their website. Only an email address was provided and the response to the requests was anonymous. This presented difficulty in trying to schedule a meeting with the IMF. It was also a display of the impersonal nature with which the IMF presents itself. It was only with the help of one of the GTI organisations that we were given the name of the contact person at the IMF headquarters and she was more concerned about how we found her contact details than in facilitating access. The response of the IMF to our requests was simply to visit the link where all publicly available information was posted. This response sends out the message that requests need not be submitted to the IMF because all that the public needs to know is on the website. After visiting the link, some of the information was available but there was no schedule of upcoming Article IV missions to South Africa.

The African Development Bank (AfDB)

A little while before submitting the requests, the information disclosure policy of the AfDB had been reviewed to permit disclosure of minutes of Board Meetings; this was one of three requests submitted to them. A new CAS was to be developed sometime in 2005 and the other requests requested a copy of the current CAS and the public consultation process for the new CAS.

The AfDB does not have an office in South Africa and at the time of submitting the three requests their website was being revamped. It was therefore necessary to telephone the office to find out how to go about requesting information. After being advised by a staff member in Tunis who to address the requests to, the requests went completely unacknowledged and so was the letter requesting a telephonic interview. The staff member also advised that the Office of the President in the country would be able to deal with requests relating to the Bank. This turned out to be untrue as is elaborated upon later in the report.

Understandably, it may not be feasible to have offices in every country of operation. However, in this case distance proved to be an obstacle to accessing information because even the local counterpart expected to hold the information was unable to offer any assistance.

The European Investment Bank (EIB)

The EIB office in Luxembourg which processed our requests provided us with the timetable for its disclosure policy review which began in 2005. Our participation was also welcomed. However, the EIB did not disclose the requested loan contract shifting this decision and responsibility to the government. While this was in accordance with its policy, the fact that the EIB is a signatory to the agreement means that it should have gone further to provide legal grounds for non-disclosure. Therefore termed the provisions of the EIB policy unsatisfactory.

The Ministry of Finance

This is the only government body that required payment of a request fee of ZAR 35 (approximately US$6). Only two out of the seven requests submitted resulted in full disclosure. In one case the Ministry provided the wrong document. The Ministry of Finance defended their mute response to the remaining requests saying that they were still following the internal protocol that accompanies such requests, which according to the staff included consulting with the respective IFI. It is worth noting that this process had gone beyond the 30-day response period without any communication to the requester either explaining the status of the requests or requesting an extension. The silent delay already created doubts that the documents would ever be disclosed. During the open discussions at the interview, we shared the mixed responses from the IFIs which had received the same requests. This may have reduced their chances of disclosure because of the negative responses from the IFIs that the Ministry staff came to learn about. The lack of a formal response from the Ministry to date led us to surmise that the Ministry may not have found any grounds in the PAIA for non-disclosure and they did not want to act in a manner that was inconsistent with the IFIs.

During the interview with the Ministry of Finance, the official admitted that two of the disclosed documents were accidentally disclosed through internal oversight. This was after we had explained that the World Bank had refused to disclose the information. The official admitted that the information had actually been sent to us by mistake and by the time they realised this, it was too late. What transpired internally was that the information officer forwarded the request by email to her colleague who was then supposed to look for the information and then pass the information to her. She would then examine the legalities around either disclosing or withholding the information before reaching a decision. Unfortunately, this protocol was not followed and when the colleague at the Ministry received the request from the Information Officer, which included our details, he promptly responded to us directly with the information.

Inasmuch as internal procedures were breached, the issue is whether the documents that were disclosed were exempt from disclosure from a legal standpoint. In this case it seems to have been more of a bureaucratic violation than a legal one because the requester only came to learn of the internal process during the interview, which was after the information had been disclosed. In addition, the same documents were disclosed in some of the other participating countries, which rather undermined what initially appeared to be a commendable sense of compliance by the Ministry to its legal responsibilities under PAIA.

The Department of Environmental Affairs and Tourism

Aide Memoires were requested from the Department but the official tasked with dealing with the request never disclosed the documents. Rather, he kept calling our partner organisation to ask them why they could not ask the World Bank for the documents. The numerous phone calls did not constitute a legally valid response according to PAIA. The official admitted that the Department had the information but he thought it best to request it directly from the Bank. When asked to offer a formal response to the request from the Department or personally ask the World Bank office if he could disclose the information, he evaded the request. It was not possible to secure an appointment with the official.

The Presidency

Unfortunately, not only did this office not respond to the requests but during the interview, distanced itself from holding such information, contrary to what we had been told by the AfDB heaquarters. On hearing the nature of the requests which were related to Board meetings and the CAS, the official from the Presidency said that the Ministry of Finance was probably better suited to handle such requests. Still, the official asked us to re-submit the requests. This was done and no acknowledgment was received or notification that the requests were transferred to another department. This did not constitute a justified response.

South African National Parks (SANParks)

SANParks is not a government Ministry but a public body. The disclosure of Aide Memoires by SANParks, which could not be disclosed by the local World Bank office, turned out to be the success story out of all the requests: the domestic law offered an opportunity to obtain IFI-related documents. It started with an email acknowledgement of the request which was quickly followed by a phone call from an official to clarify the request. The requester was even informed of an upcoming World Bank appraisal mission that would result in another Aide Memoire. Once the new Aide Memoire had been released, it was promptly sent to the requester alongside the preceding Aide Memoire. Not only was the information disclosed but also the institution emerged as a leader in establishing best practice for dealing with requests and requesters. The staff of SANParks stood out from all the rest by the professionalism exercised in dealing with the requesters and the swift handling of the requests.

During the interview, the staff was pleased to learn of their good performance compared to other institutions. The staff attributed this to their organisational culture which encourages openness and interaction with the public thereby enabling them to comply with PAIA. They also provided a copy of their internal policy for implementing PAIA. They simply felt that they had no reason to withhold the information.

Results by type of document

Overall, seven requests had a positive outcome where some, if not all, information requested was received. Seventeen requests had a negative outcome with the institutions either denying the information on the basis of their disclosure policy or simply not responding to the request. A full list of all the requests is included in Annex I.

Key documents related to policy decisions as well as project-specific information that affect borrowing countries were requested from the IFIs and the respective government partners.

Minutes and/or summaries of Board Meetings

Minutes of discussion at the latest meeting of the Executive Directors of the IMF were requested. Concluding statements made by IMF staff members after visiting member countries, referred to as Article IV missions, which can be made public on a voluntary basis were also requested, including a full schedule of upcoming missions. The IMF provided a weblink which contained the minutes and concluding statements of Article IV missions but a schedule of upcoming missions was not provided. The Ministry of Finance did not respond to this request.

The documents requested from the local World Bank office and the Ministry of Finance were: Summary of Board Meetings on World Bank Disclosure Policy: Additional Issues, November 18, 2004 and the latest written statement presented to the Board from the Country Executive Director on the meeting where the present CAS was discussed.

These documents were disclosed by the Ministry of Finance but denied by the World Bank office who quoted the World Bank Policy on Information Disclosure and the World Bank Disclosure Policy: Additional Issues. Follow-up consolidated report (Revised).

Requests for summaries of AfDB Board Meetings went unheeded from both the AfDB and the Presidency.

Country Assistance Strategies (CASs)

The AfDB current Country Strategy Paper for South Africa could not be obtained as no response was received from the Bank and the South African Presidency. A schedule for the consultation process of the new Country Strategy Paper was also requested with no response.

Information Disclosure Policy Reviews

The timetable for the consultative process for the Review of the EIB's Public Information Policy launched in the 1st quarter of 2005 was requested. This information was provided by the EIB but not by the Ministry of Finance. The EIB invited our participation, which was done collectively by the GTI founding organisations.

31

Aide Memoires

Aide Memoires are project reports developed throughout the life of a project and are normally issued after country appraisal missions by the World Bank to the borrowing country. Aide Memoires were requested for three projects, namely; the Municipal Financial Technical Assistance Project, the Maloti-Drakensburg Transfrontier Conservation and Development Project and the Greater Addo Elephant National Park Project. Tied to the last project, records of surveys/audits of outstanding land claims lodged with the Land Claims Commission in respect of land to be incorporated into the park were also requested.

Instead of providing the Aide Memoires for the Municipal Financial Technical Assistance Project, the Ministry of Finance provided the loan agreement. The Department of Environmental Affairs did not respond to the request for the Maloti-Drakensburg Transfrontier Conservation and Development Project Aide Memoires. SANParks disclosed the two most recent Aide Memoirs and transferred the request on land claims to the Land Claims Commission because it did not hold the records. This was in compliance with the law. However no response was provided by the Commission.

Loan contracts

A copy of the loan contract for the EIB-funded Mozambique-South Africa Natural Gas Project was requested from the EIB and the Ministry of Finance. This document was not disclosed. According to the EIB response, it could only be disclosed with the consent of the client, in this case the Government of South Africa. The Ministry of Finance never responded to the request despite promising feedback during the interview.

South Africa: Conclusions and recommendations

Four main obstacles to accessing IFI information emerged from the requesting process and the interviews conducted with officials.

Centralisation of decision-making on information disclosure in IFIs

This was experienced at two levels: where an institution had no local office and where an institution with a local office did not have full autonomy in dealing with requests. The AfDB is an example of the former while the IFC is an example of the latter, whereby it was clear that the head offices in Washington D.C had the last word on the requests we submitted, which implied that decision-making on information disclosure is still centralised even when the requests related to South Africa. The requesting procedure of these IFIs is complicated by the lack of information on where requests should be submitted. No contact details which refer to a particular office are provided by the IFC.

This is not a problem of local institutions because of the provisions of the South African FOIA, the PAIA, which not only requires the appointment of Information Officers but also requires a clear roadmap for the public for submitting requests. The IFIs need to include such provisions in their disclosure policies to facilitate access to information.

The problem of mute refusals[41]

South Africa had the highest rate of mute refusals in all five countries. Weaknesses in IFI disclosure policies mean that IFIs have no formal legal obligation to respond to a requester. However, this is not the case with PAIA. The World Bank and the Presidency claimed not to have received some of the requests despite the requester having submitted the requests by fax and email to ensure that they were received. Although this explanation was accepted in good faith, the fact that the requester never received any communication resulted in the outcome mute refusal being assigned. As stated earlier, there was no communication from the AfDB to the requests, to the follow-ups made and to the request for an interview. Other requests which were received by the Ministry of Finance and the Department of Environmental Affairs and Tourism were not responded to.

The fact that PAIA requires institutions to respond to requests with disclosure or reasons for non-disclosure within 30 days, unless a formal extension is requested, means that the law is violated repeatedly. Strict measures to ensure compliance not only need to be put in place but officials need to take the right to know seriously and cultivate a culture that promotes open information sharing.

Poor sanctions for non-compliance both in IFIs and at the national level

Although appeals were not conducted in the pilot phase, the problem of mute refusals described above points to weaknesses in the system, whereby officials are able to deny information and simply get away with it. By looking at the appeal systems in place, there are glaring weaknesses in the set-up of these mechanisms which ought to be practically tested in future. The South African FOIA has provisions for internal appeals to the institution that did not provide the information but this applies when a formal refusal has been provided. Thereafter, a requester can proceed to court, a lengthy and expensive option.

Even in cases where formal refusals were provided, no option of appeal was presented to the requester implying they had to accept the fact that they could not get the information or acquaint themselves with the legal procedure for appeal on their own. The IFIs appeal system is not clearly understood by the staff charged with dealing with requests as demonstrated during the interview with the World Bank staff that referred the requester to the World Bank staff who drafted the policy. Access to justice is therefore compromised.

If both IFIs and government bodies provide legal grounds for refusals to requesters outlining the options available to the requester, then they not only demonstrate the extent to which they seek to promote the right to know but they also further the understanding of the scope of what information is publicly available and open themselves to scrutiny. This of course goes hand in hand with the existence of a rapid, inexpensive and independent appeal system.

General attitudes amongst officials

There was a general feeling amongst government staff that if IFI information is classified as confidential in an IFI disclosure policy, then regardless of whether the national FOIA allows for disclosure or not, some degree of caution should be exercised with such requests. During the interviews, the staff of the two government agencies, which disclosed information that had been denied by the World Bank, said that had they known that the World Bank refused to disclose the information they may have acted differently. It is not clear whether this meant non-disclosure, but third party confidentiality consideration was inferred.

The manner in which the requests were dealt with internally in the Ministry of Finance stems from the attitude of the officials to disclosure. The internal procedures in place seem to be designed to 'protect' information and to obstruct instead of encourage disclosure. The high level of caution in these procedures is typical of such a critical government agency. However, in the case of these requests there is a thin line between prudence on the one hand, and suspicion and egregious secrecy, which goes against the spirit of the right to know, on the other.

Numerous efforts to secure an interview with the Department of Environmental Affairs and Tourism, and the International Finance Corporation were unsuccessful. These were the same institutions that did not respond to the information requests that were submitted to them. In general, it was much easier to secure interviews with institutions where the name and contact details of the Information Officer was known.

The staff of the World Bank and SANParks, however, stood out from all the rest because of the professionalism exercised in dealing with the requesters and the swift handling of the requests. As a result, SANParks displayed the best open practice among the local bodies and the World Bank, which admitted that more still needs to be done, and handled requests better than the other IFIs. Attitude is critical in promoting the right to know and cannot be enforced by a FOIA or IFI disclosure policy.

4. Conclusion

The study provided valuable information regarding IFI information and important lessons for our future work. A summary of experiences in Argentina, Bulgaria, Mexico, Slovakia and South Africa revealed the following:

- A generally high level of opacity surrounding the disclosure of information related to IFIs, with poor disclosure of information;
- Incidences of low quality of information disclosure, with cases of incomplete information being provided with minimal detail, delays and other practical obstacles to disclosure;
- A lack of responsiveness in dealing with requesters and a poor commitment to promoting the right to know, with a substantial proportion of requests simply being ignored;
- Inconsistencies in the interpretation and implementation of disclosure policies resulting in different outcomes for the same requests;
- Inadequate communication and information sharing between IFIs and borrowing governments and centralisation of decision-making regarding information disclosure in the IFI headquarters;
- FOIAs provide an alternative avenue for access to IFI information but domestic implementation challenges persist and strict internal procedures are necessary to ensure adequate compliance;
- Bulgaria had the highest success rate in getting information but Slovakia produced standard-setting practices in FOIA implementation. Performance was generally poor in Argentina, Mexico and Slovakia;
- The World Bank was the most responsive IFI and corrective measures have been embraced by the IADB office in Argentina and public bodies to improve transparency and accountability following the results of this study.

IFI information disclosure policies need to take a number of progressive steps towards transparency and accountability. Our recommendations for proactive disclosure of IFI policies, which are based on the findings of the study, as well as the principles of the GTI Transparency Charter, demand the following minimum disclosure requirements:

- IFI policies must regard the right of access to information as a fundamental human right. Their disclosure policies should be based on the principle of public interest accountability, in line with domestic FOIA, and the public must be notified of upcoming consultations. Further, all formal meetings with decision-making powers should be open to the public;
- IFI policies must operate from a presumption of disclosure which means that all information held should be disclosed, subject to narrowly defined exceptions which are explicit and indicate precise harm that would result from disclosure;
- IFI policies should provide clear and detailed procedures for processing requests which support and facilitate equal access, regardless of location, education or language. These include, among other things, contact details which accommodate requests submitted in different modes, clear response time-frames, routine disclosure of basic information and written reasons for refusals;
- IFI policies should provide for the right to appeal refusals through a rapid, free internal appeal as well as an independent mechanism;
- IFI policies should undergo a regular and comprehensive review aimed at promoting freedom of information.

Endnotes

1   The GTI is a network of civil society organisations promoting openness in IFIs, such as the World Bank, the International Monetary Fund, the European Investment Bank and Regional Development Banks. More information on the GTI is available on http://www.ifitransparency.org

2   The selected IFIs were the International Monetary Fund; the International Bank for Reconstruction and Development and the International Finance Corporation of the World Bank Group; the European Investment Bank; the European Bank for Reconstruction and Development; the African Development Bank; the Inter American Development Bank and the Andean Development Corporation. Various national government agencies implementing IFI projects or known to hold IFI-related information were selected in each country.

3   Jong-Il You (2002) 'The Bretton Woods Institutions: Evolution, Reform and Change' in *Governing Globalization – Issues and Institutions* edited by Nayyar, D. p.219. OUP, New York.

4   The draft Charter is available on http://ifitransparency.org/doc/charter_en.pdf

5   A mute refusal means that no information was disclosed and no formal refusal was provided.

6   A two-month response time was agreed upon for the study because of the lack of specified time-frames in the IFI disclosure policies.

7   The request was submitted to the IFC office in Moscow by the Slovak organisation because there was no local country office.

8   See full article on http://www.ifitransparency.org/resources.shtml?x=44973

9   This case study report has been written by Víctor Ricco, Paula Granada and Angeles Pereira. victor@cedha.org, paula@cedha.org.ar and angeles@cedha.org.ar

10 Articles 14 and 75 subparagraph 22. The latter states that 'every person has the right to request, receive and impart information' a tenor of article 13 of the American Convention on Human Rights. (Our translation.)

11 At present, the bill has been already been discussed by both chambers. However, reforms incorporated after the first presentation of the bill have been strongly criticised by many Argentine NGOs. For further information, see www.adc.org.ar and www.cels.org.ar

12 The World Bank has a regional office in the Argentina federal capital, which serves Argentina, Chile, Paraguay and Uruguay.

13 In Argentina, the IADB representative office is located in the federal capital of the country and has a special coordinator in charge of access to public information. (Our translation.)

14 In Argentina, the CAF office operates within the national Ministry of Economy and Production. It has an office of public relations with international credit bodies (*Dirección de Relaciones con Organismos internacionales de Crédito*) meant to articulate the relationship between the Argentina government and the main IFIs (World Bank, IADB, CAF and FONPLATA).

15 This case study report has been written by Nikolay Marekov. mareq@aip-bg.org

16 For example, in the process of compiling a handbook for the administration last year, we requested the internal rules on information provision from all Ministries and some other executive agencies. AIP also conducts Freedom of Information trainings for the central and local administration.

17 See http://siteresources.worldbank.org/INTBULGARIA/Resources/CAS2002web.pdf

18 Programmatic adjustment loans, supporting the administrative reform in Bulgaria

19 http://www1.worldbank.org/operations/disclosure/documents/TranslationFramework.pdf

20 As seen from some articles in the newspaper one of them is available in English and can be found at: http://www.standartnews.com/archive/2005/05/05/english/business/

21 Sent to the European Commission regarding the issues to be resolved concerning the NHWC, EIB's view on the EIA and the list of

documents to be provided by the Bulgarian Ministry of Environment and Water

22 More information in English is available at http://www.zazemiata.org/bw/radnevo/index_en.php

23 http://www.ebrd.com/new/pressrel/2001/01 jun151x.htm

24 Launched in 2000, ISPA is one of the three European Union financial instruments to assist the candidate countries in the preparation for accession. It provides assistance for infrastructure projects in the European Union priority fields of environment and transport.

25 The official stand of the EIB in relation to Financial contract FI No 20.60 for the construction of Trakia Highway

26 Letter of the European Investment Bank REF No. H4(2005)A/1648 from 24/01/2005 in relation to the construction of a National Hazardous Waste Center in the region of Radnevo

27 The Council of Ministers keeps a register of state and municipal concessions, which is available online since December, 2005. The register does not contain full-text contracts.

28 More information about the International Right to Know Day ceremony in Bulgaria is available at: http://www.righttoknowday.net/index_eng.htm

29 The Charter is available on http://ifitransparency.org/doc/charter_en.pdf

30 For example, the European Commission responded that 'the documents you requested are the documents of the EIB

31 One of the most striking examples of this was the Bulgarian Ministry of Justice's decision to withhold access to a list of projects in support of the judicial reform in Bulgaria financed by international donors. The request was part of the Freedom of Information Monitoring survey administered by the Open Society Justice Initiative and conducted in 16 countries in 2004. The Ministry refused to provide access to the requested information because they lacked the consent of the donors.

32 This report has been written by Issa Luna Pla. issa.luna@limac.org.mx

33 http://www1.worldbank.org/operations/discloure/documents/disclosurepolicy.pdf

34 This case study report has been written by Peter Mihok. mihok_peter@yahoo.com

35 More on the background on this is contained in the NGOs Issue Paper: *EIB loan contracts for public projects in Slovakia on the internet.* CEE Bankwatch Network 2005. http://bankwatch.org/documents/railways_contract_sk_03_05.pdf

36 Outside of this project, we submitted a complaint to the European Union Ombudsman on the fact that another finance contract of 1999 between the EIB and the state owned railway company was considered confidential by the EIB despite being disclosed by the Ministry of Transport and the Office of the Government. The complaint to the European Union Ombudsman was sent in March 2006.

37 This case study report has been written by Catherine Musuva. catherine@idasact.org.za

38 Jagwanth, S. (2002). 'The right to information as a leverage right', in *The right to know, the right to live: access to information and socio-economic justice,* Calland, R. & Tilley, A. (eds.) Open Democracy Advice Centre, Cape Town.

39 Open Democracy Advice Centre (2006) *Five years on…The right to know in South Africa.* Open Democracy Advice Centre, Cape Town.

40 Reference was made to para. 83 of the World Bank Policy on Disclosure of Information which states: 'Proceedings of the Board of Executive Directors and committees thereof are, under the Board's Rules of Procedure, confidential. Thus, unless disclosure is approved by the Board, documents prepared for the consideration or review and approval of the Executive Directors (other than those specifically made publicly available as provided for in this statement) are not publicly available.'

Reference was also made to *World Bank Disclosure Policy: Additional Issues. Follow-up consolidated report (Revised), 2005* to emphasise the non disclosure of Board minutes.

41 Mute refusal represents all instances where the requested information was neither provided nor was a formal written response provided to the requester within the monitoring period.

Annex 1: Requests by country

ARGENTINA

Request #	Requestor	Requestee	Question	Full outcome
RQ01	CEDHA	World Bank Group	Summary of Board Meetings on World Bank Disclosure Policy: Additional Issues, November 18, 2004.	Information received
RQ02	CEDHA	World Bank Group	Latest written statement presented to the Board from the Country Executive Director on the meeting where the present CAS was discussed.	Information received
RQ03	CEDHA	World Bank Group	PO N° 88220: Copy of the Risk Management Scheme document- Copy of the EIA document of the project.	Information received
RQ04	IDEAS	World Bank Group	PO N° 70374: The list of the sub-projects involved in this major project, including a copy of the executive summary documents about Cordoba Province projects.	Mute refusal
RQ05	IDEAS	World Bank Group	ARPE N° 73578: Copy of the EIA document submitted in Spanish and a summarised copy of the last advance document of the project (state report) with a list of the sub-projects involved in the main project.	Mute refusal
RQ06	CEDHA	IMF	Minutes of discussion at the latest meeting of the Executive Directors of the IMF.	Unable to submit
RQ07	CEDHA	IMF	Concluding Statements from the most recent Article IV mission and a full schedule of upcoming Article IV missions to Argentina.	Unable to submit
RQ08	CEDHA	IADB	Copy of the general document concerning the sub-project '12,000' viviendas' developed in Cordoba Province, specifically the part regarding objectives, and a copy of the report presented by the government.	Mute refusal
RQ09	IDEAS	IADB	AR N° 0163: Copy of the EIA document aproved by the CMA on 05/12/2005. Information about Cordoba sub-projects.	Mute refusal
RQ10	CEDHA	IIRSA	Copy of the document explaining the mechanism used to monitor and audit the development of projects in both countries and copy transferrend of the EIA document.	Transferred
RQ11	CEDHA	IIRSA	Copy of the document explaining the mechanism used to monitor and audit the development of project in both countries and copy of the EIA document.	Mute refusal
RQ12	CEDHA	IFC	Country Impact Review and Country Impact Notes for Argentina	Information received
RQ13	CEDHA	IADB	Current Argentina Country Strategy Paper 2003 – 2005	Mute refusal
RQ14	CEDHA	Ministry of Economy	Summary of Board Meetings on World Bank Disclosure Policy: Additional Issues, November 18, 2004	Mute Refusal
RQ15	CEDHA	Ministry of Economy	Latest written statement presented to the Board from the Country Executive Director on the meeting where the present CAS was discussed.	Mute Refusal
RQ16	CEDHA	Ministry of Economy	PO N° 88220: Copy of the Risk Management Scheme document- Copy of the EIA document of the project.	Refusal to Acept
RQ17	IDEAS	National Council of Women	PO N° 70374: The list of the sub-projects involved in this major project, including a copy of the executive summary documents about Cordoba Province projects.	Unable to submit
RQ18	IDEAS	Ministry of Labor, Employment & Human Resources	ARPE N° 73578: Copy of the EIA document submitted in Spanish and a summarised copy of the last advance document of the project (state report) with a list of the sub-projects involved in the main project.	Mute refusal
RQ19	CEDHA	Ministry of Economy	Minutes of discussion at the latest meeting of the Executive Directors of the IMF	Unable to submit
RQ20	CEDHA	Ministry of Economy	Concluding Statements from the most recent Article IV mission and a full schedule of upcoming Article IV missions	Unable to submit

Request #	Requestor	Requestee	Question	Full outcome
RQ21	CEDHA	Ministry of the Solidarity- Social Promotion Secretary.	Copy of the general document concerning the sub-project '12,000' viviendas' developed in Cordoba Province, specifically the part regarding objectives, and a copy of the report presented by the government.	Mute refusal
RQ22	IDEAS	Ministry of the Solidarity- Social Promotion Secretary.	AR N° 0163: Copy of the EIA document approved by the CMA on 05/12/2005. Information about Cordoba sub-projects.	Mute refusal
RQ23	CEDHA	Ministry of Federal Planification, Public Invertion and Service Secretary.	Copy of the document explaining the mechanism used to monitor and audit the development of project in both countries and copy of the EIA document.	Information received
RQ24	CEDHA	Ministry of Federal Planification, Public Invertion and Service Secretary.	Copy of the document explaning the mechanism used to monitor and audit the development of project in both countries and copy of the EIA document.	Information received

BULGARIA				
RQ01	AIP	WB	Summary of Board Meetings on World Bank Disclosure Policy: Additional Issues, November 18, 2004	Information received
RQ02	AIP	WB	Latest written statement presented to the Board from the Country Executive Director on CAS	Information received
RQ03	ZZ	WB	List of documents (correspondence) between the Bulgarian Government and the World Bank in relation to PAL	Refusal
RQ04	ZZ	WB	The matrixes of all PAL projects for Bulgaria	Information received
RQ05	ZZ	WB	The reports from all PAL projects for Bulgaria	Information received
RQ06	AIP	IMF	IMF report adopted in 2004 covering the long-term relationships between the Fund and Bulgaria	Information received
RQ07	AIP	IMF	The concluding statements and assessments following the Article IV consultations with Bulgaria in 2004	Information received
RQ08	ZZ	EBRD	Concession contract between the Municipality of Sofia and International Water/United Utilities + amendments	Mute refusal
RQ09	ZZ	EBRD	List of all projects funded or co-funded by the Kozloduy International Decomissioning Support Fund	Mute refusal
RQ10	AIP	EIB	Official stand of the EIB in relation to financial contract FI No 20.60 for the construction of Trakia Highway	Refusal
RQ11	AIP	EIB	Letter of the European Investment Bank REF No. – H4(2005)A/1648 from 24/01/2005 (NHWC)	Refusal
RQ12	AIP	IFC	List of approved IFC projects for Bulgaria	Mute refusal
RQ13	AIP	WB	Information policy in Bulgarian	Information not held
RQ14	AIP	MinFin	Summary of Board Meetings on World Bank Disclosure Policy: Additional Issues, November 18, 2004	Information received
RQ15	AIP	MinFin	Latest written statement presented to the Board from the Country Executive Director on CAS	Mute refusal
RQ16	ZZ	CoM	List of documents (corersponndence) between the Bulgarian Government and the WB in relation to PAL	Incomplete answer
RQ17	ZZ	CoM	The matrixes of all PAL projects for Bulgaria	Incomplete answer
RQ18	ZZ	CoM	The reports from all PAL projects for Bulgaria	Incomplete answer
RQ19	AIP	MinFin	IMF report adopted in 2004 covering the long-term relationships between the Fund and Bulgaria	Information received
RQ20	AIP	MinFin	The concluding statements and assessments following the Article IV consultations with Bulgaria in 2004	Information received
RQ21	ZZ	CoM	Concession contract between the Municipality of Sofia and International Water/United Utilities + amendments	Incomplete answer
RQ22	ZZ	MEER	List of all projects funded or co-funded by the Kozloduy International Decomissioning Support Fund	Information received
RQ23	AIP	MRRB	Official stand of the EIB in relation to financial contract FI No 20.60 for the construction of Trakia Highway	Information not held

Request #	Requestor	Requestee	Question	Full outcome
RQ24	AIP	MOEW	Letter of the European Investment Bank REF No. – H4(2005)A/1648 from 24/01/2005 (NHWC)	Mute refusal

MEXICO

Request #	Requestor	Requestee	Question	Full outcome
RQ01	LIMAC	World Bank Group	Summary of Board Meetings on World Bank Disclosure Policy: Additional Issues, November 18, 2004	Refusal
RQ02	LIMAC	World Bank Group	Latest written statement presented to the Board from the Country Executive Director on the meeting where the present CAS was discussed	Refusal
RQ03	LIMAC	World Bank Group	Last Country Review Portfolio Review due in Mexico	Refusal
RQ04	LIMAC	World Bank Group	Documents on the supervision process of the project execution on'Equidad de Genero' loan number 7022-ME implemented by the Women National Institute	Refusal
RQ05	LIMAC	World Bank Group	Minutes related to the election process of the state of Guanajuato for the Sistema de Compras Gubernamentales and documents where policies for the selection of entities is established.	Information not held
RQ06	LIMAC	IMF	Minutes of discussion at the latest meeting of the Executive Directors of the IMF	Refusal to accept
RQ07	LIMAC	IMF	Concluding Statements from the most recent Article IV mission and a full schedule of upcoming Article IV missions	Refusal to accept
RQ08	LIMAC	IADB	Copy of original documents produced during the data collection for the ICP applied in Mexico for the Plan Puebla Panama prior to systemising	Incomplete answer
RQ09	LIMAC	IADB	Reports of finalised projects finished in the last 10 years (e.g. 1072, 1252,1256) and any ex post evaluation of them	Information not held
RQ10	LIMAC	IMF	Information related to the Shorebank Advisory Services Company in Chicago from the project MIF/AT-244	Refusal to accept
RQ11	LIMAC	IMF	Information related to the Guanajuato World Trade Commission Company (COFOCE) and contact information regarding project MIF/AT-548	Refusal to accept
RQ12	LIMAC	IFC	Country Impact Review and Country Impact Notes	Information not held
RQ13	LIMAC	IADB	Current country strategy paper	Incomplete answer
RQ14	LIMAC	Ministry of Finance	Summary of Board Meetings on World Bank Disclosure Policy: Additional Issues, November 18, 2004	Referred
RQ15	LIMAC	Ministry of Finance	Latest written statement presented to the Board from the Country Executive Director on the meeting where the present CAS was discussed	Incomplete answer
RQ16	LIMAC	Ministry of Exterior	Last Country Review Portfolio Review due in Mexico	Referred
RQ17	LIMAC	Ministry of Finance	Documents on the supervision process of the project execution on'Equidad de Genero' loan number 7022-ME implemented by the Women National Institute	Information received
RQ18	LIMAC	Ministry of Finance	Minutes related to the election process of the state of Guanajuato for the Sistema de Compras Gubernamentales and documents where policies for the selection of entities is established.	Referred
RQ19	LIMAC	Ministry of Finance	Minutes of discussion at the latest meeting of the Executive Directors of the IMF	Referred
RQ20	LIMAC	Ministry of Finance	Concluding Statements from the most recent Article IV mission and a full schedule of upcoming Article IV missions	Information received
RQ21	LIMAC	President's Office	Copy of original documents produced during the data collection for the ICP applied in Mexico for the Plan Puebla Panama prior to systemising	Referred
RQ22	LIMAC	Ministry of Finance	Reports of finalised projects finished in the last 10 years (e.g. 1072, 1252,1256) and any ex post evaluation of them	Referred
RQ23	LIMAC	Ministry of Finance	Information related to the Shorebank Advisory Services Company in Chicago from the project MIF/AT-244	Referred
RQ24	LIMAC	Ministry of Finance	Information related to the Guanajuato World Trade Commission Company (COFOCE) and contact information regarding project MIF/AT-548	Referred

Request #	Requestor	Requestee	Question	Full outcome
SLOVAKIA				
RQ01	CEPA	World Bank Bratislava office	Summary of Board Meeting on World Bank Disclosure Policy: Additional Issues, (from November 18, 2004)	Refusal
RQ02	CEPA	World Bank Bratislava office	Copy of the statement of Mr. Roger Grawe, which was presented at the Board when CPS for Slovakia for 2005-07 was discussed last year.	Refusal
RQ03	Uplift	World Bank Bratislava office	Copies of a) Aide Memoires documents and b) contracts made with the relevant authorities of the Slovak republic related to these projects: 1. Social Benefits Reform Administration Project	Partial access
RQ04	Uplift	World Bank Bratislava office	Copies of a) Aide Memoires documents and b) contracts made with the relevant authorities of the Slovak republic related to these projects: 2. Health Project & Health Sector Modernisation Support Technical Assistance Project	Partial access
RQ05	Uplift	IFC Regional office in Moscow	Copies of Aide Memoires documents related to project 'Samsung Calex', financed from the GEF.	Mute refusal
RQ06	CEPA	IMF	Copy of the document 'Minutes of discussion from the meeting of the Executive Directors from the meeting where the IMF Executive Board concluded 2004 Article IV Consultation with the Slovak Republic.	Refusal
RQ07	CEPA	IMF	Schedule of upcoming Article IV missions into Slovakia	Partial access
RQ08	Uplift	EBRD	Timetable of the next process of consultations with civic organisations about the next CAS for Slovakia.	Partial access
RQ09	Uplift	EBRD	Non-technical summary of the Environmental Impact Assessment for the project Kronospan (Presov, Slovakia).	Partial access
RQ10	CEPA	EIB	Non-technical Summary of the Environmental Impact Assessment of the project 'Kosicka bridge in Slovakia' in the English language.	Partial access
RQ11	CEPA	EIB	Copy of the Finance Contract between the Slovak republic and the European Investment Bank on the project Slovak republic – Motorway and expressway programme – D/1 Svinia – Pre?ov, R/1 Rudno nad Hronom – ?arnovica.	Refusal
RQ12	CEPA	IFC Regional office in Moscow	Copy of the documents 'Country Impact Review' (CIR) and 'Country Impact Notes' (CIN) for the Slovak Republic.	Mute refusal
RQ13	Uplift	EBRD	Copy of the document (actual) CAS for the Slovak Republic.	Information received
RQ14	CEPA	Ministry of Finance	Copy of document Summary of Board Meeting on World Bank Disclosure Policy: Additional Issues, (from November 18, 2004)	Information not held
RQ15	CEPA	Ministry of Finance	Copy of the statement of Mr. Roger Grawe, which was presented at the Board when CPS for Slovakia for 2005-07 was discussed last year.	Information not held
RQ16	Uplift	Ministry of Labour	Copies of a) Aide Memoires documents and b) contracts made with the relevant authorities of the Slovak Republic related to these projects: 1. Social Benefits Reform Administration Project	Partial access
RQ17	Uplift	Ministry of Health	Copies of a) Aide Memoires documents and b) contracts made with the relevant authorities of the Slovak Republic related to these projects: 2. Health Project & Health Sector Modernisation Support Technical Assistance Project	Partial access
RQ18	Uplift	Ministry of Environment	Copies of Aide Memoires documents related to project 'Samsung Calex', financed from the GEF.	Transferred/referred
RQ19	CEPA	Ministry of Finance	Copy of the document 'Minutes of discussion from the meeting of the Executive Directors' from the meeting where the IMF Executive Board concluded 2004 Article IV Consultation with the Slovak Republic.	Refusal
RQ20	CEPA	Ministry of Finance	Schedule of upcoming Article IV mission into Slovakia	Information not held
RQ21	Uplift	Ministry of Finance	Timetable of the next process of consultations with civic organisations about the next CAS for Slovakia.	Information not held
RQ22	Uplift	Ministry of Environment	Non-technical summary of the Environmental Impact Assessment for the project Kronospan (Presov, Slovakia).	Information received
RQ23	CEPA	Ministry of Environment	Non-technical Summary of the Environmental Impact Assessment of the project 'Kosicka bridge in Slovakia' in the English language.	Information not held

Request #	Requestor	Requestee	Question	Full outcome
RQ24	CEPA	Ministry of Finance	Copy of the Finance Contract between the Slovak republic and the European Investment Bank on the project Slovak republic – Motorway and expressway programme – D/1 Svinia – Pre?ov, R/1 Rudno nad Hronom – ?arnovica.	Information received

SOUTH AFRICA

Request #	Requestor	Requestee	Question	Full outcome
RQ01	IDASA	World Bank Group	Summary of Board Meetings on World Bank Disclosure Policy: Additional Issues, November 18, 2004	Refusal
RQ02	IDASA	World Bank Group	Latest written statement presented to the Board from the Country Executive Director on the meeting where the present CAS was discussed	Refusal
RQ03	ODAC	World Bank Group	Aide Memoire relevant to the Greater Addo National Park Project, Records of surveys/audits of outstanding land claims lodged with the Land Claims Commission in respect of land to be incoporated into the park.	Mute refusal
RQ04	ODAC	World Bank Group	Aide Memoire relevant to the Municipal Financial Technical Assistance Project	Mute refusal
RQ05	ODAC	World Bank Group	Aide Memoire relevant to the Maloti-Drakensburg Transfrontier Conservation and Development Project	Mute refusal
RQ06	IDASA	IMF	Minutes of discussion at the latest meeting of the Executive Directors of the IMF	Information received
RQ07	IDASA	IMF	Concluding Statements from the most recent Article IV mission. and a full schedule of upcoming Article IV missions to South Africa	Incomplete answer
RQ08	ODAC	AfDB	Consultative/Participation process timetable for the South Africa Country Strategy to be developed in 2005.	Mute refusal
RQ09	ODAC	AfDB	Summary of Board Meetings held in 2005	Mute refusal
RQ10	IDASA	EIB	Timetable for the consultative process for the Review of the EIB's Public Information Policy launched in the 1st quarter of 2005.	Information received
RQ11	IDASA	EIB	Loan contract for the Mozambique-South Africa Natural Gas Project	Refusal
RQ12	IDASA	IFC	Country Impact Review and Country Impact Notes for South Africa	Incomplete answer
RQ13	ODAC	AfDB	Current South Africa Country Strategy Paper 2003 – 2005	Mute refusal
RQ14	IDASA	Ministry of Finance	Summary of Board Meetings on World Bank Disclosure Policy: Additional Issues, November 18, 2004	Information received
RQ15	IDASA	Ministry of Finance	Latest written statement presented to the Board from the Country Executive Director on the meeting where the present CAS was discussed.	Information received
RQ16	ODAC	SANParks	Aide Memoire relevant to the Greater Addo National Park Project, Records of surveys/audits of outstanding land claims lodged with the Land Claims Commission in respect of land to be incorporated into the park.	Information received
RQ17	ODAC	Ministry of Finance	Aide Memoire relevant to the Municipal Financial Technical Assistance Project	Mute refusal
RQ18	ODAC	Ministry of Environmental Affairs & Tourism	Aide Memoire relevant to the Maloti- Drakensburg Transfrontier Conservation and Development Project	Refusal
RQ19	IDASA	Ministry of Finance	Minutes of discussion at the latest meeting of the Executive Directors of the IMF	Mute refusal
RQ20	IDASA	Ministry of Finance	Concluding Statements from the most recent Article IV mission. and a full schedule of upcoming Article IV missions to South Africa	Mute refusal
RQ21	ODAC	The Presidency	Consultative/Participation process timetable for the South Africa Country Strategy to be developed in 2005.	Mute refusal
RQ22	ODAC	The Presidency	Summary of Board Meetings held in 2005	Mute refusal
RQ23	IDASA	Ministry of Finance	Timetable for the consultative process for the Review of the EIB's Public Information Policy launched in the 1st quarter of 2005.	Mute refusal
RQ24	IDASA	Ministry of Finance	Loan contract for the Mozambique-South Africa Natural Gas Project	Mute refusal

41

Annex 2: Definitions of outcomes

Unable to submit

Unable to submit means that it was not physically possible to file the request.

It may be that you are 'unable to submit' written requests for some other reason. For example, a request sent by post is returned, an email bounces (if you are sure you have the right email address), or you can't get a fax through (if you are sure you have the right fax number), etc, then you should try to submit by another method before calling it an unable to submit.

Requestors should make three (3) attempts to submit before concluding that they were unable to submit.

Refusal to accept

Refusal to accept is when the institution actually refuses to accept the request. This would include a response that 'We do not accept requests for information'.

Refusal to accept also includes the refusal to accept a written request being delivered in person. It could also include a reply to an e-mail or fax saying that the request cannot be accepted in this format (if this is in contravention of the law). It could also include refusal to sign for a request sent by registered delivery post (when you are sure it's going to the right person or office).

If national law (FOI, administrative or other) requires that you are entitled to a registration number or reference number or receipt for submission of your request, or if you have a right to have a second copy of your request certified, and that this is normal administrative practice, then this should be asked for. Failure by the authorities to provide this can be counted as a refusal to accept.

In all cases of refusal to accept, the authority must have actively declined to accept the request.

Refusal

A refusal happens when an official says that they refuse to provide the information, whether or not they give grounds. This would include a response to hand-delivered requests such as 'I am sorry Madam, but we cannot provide that information as it is classified.' A Refusal can also be made by telephone, for example during a phone call to verify whether a written request has been received, or a phone call made at the initiative of the authority. A refusal may also come in the form of a letter, email or fax or a written document handed to the requestor.

Mute refusal

Mute refusal represents all instances where the requested information was neither provided nor was a formal written response provided to the requester within the monitoring period.

Information received (request fulfilled) (late information received)

Access is granted and the information is provided, in written or oral form. The information answers the question and is relatively complete.

Incomplete response/incomplete answer (late incomplete answer)

Information is provided but is seriously incomplete, irrelevant or in some other way unsatisfactory so that it demonstrates manifest disregard for the right of access to information.

For example, if specific information is requested and a large pile of documents is provided which does not directly provide the answer, or if the requestor is directed to a website which does not have all the information.

Partial access (late partial access)

Partial access is information which has been blacked-out or 'severed' or has had part of the information excluded on grounds provided for by the law, primarily grounds relating to the exemptions or other acceptable grounds.

Partial access is also where you are provided with one document only and where the authority clearly states that other documents/pages were withheld because of application of the exemptions; if not clearly stated, this should be classified as Incomplete answer.

One other acceptable reason for exempting information is that part of it does not relate to a private body's public function, but this must be clearly stated; if not clearly stated, this should be classified as Incomplete answer.

Transferred or referred (late transfer/ referral)

The institution provides a written or oral answer which refers the requestor to another institution, or the authority makes a transfer of the request to another institution.

Our assumption is that international standards require, at a minimum, that the requestor is referred to the body which holds the information. This is our minimum standards for the transferred/referred category. If national law provides that the request must be transferred, then this is the standard to which we hold the requestees.

You should include in this category

* Responses which are referrals if the law does not mention either referrals or transferrals;
* Responses which are referrals if the law provides for this;
* Responses which alert the requestor to transfer if the law provides for this;
* Responses coming from another authority which alert us to the fact that the request was transferred.

Information not held

If the authority answers that it does not hold the information and does not know who holds the information, we record it as information not held.

Annex 3: Outcomes by country

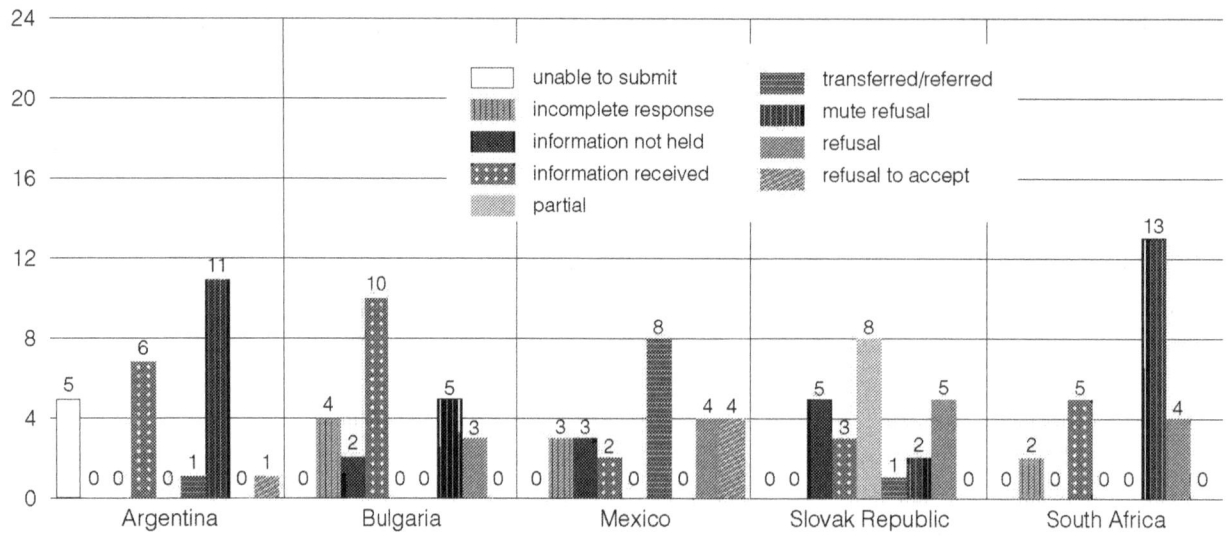

Legend:
- unable to submit
- incomplete response
- information not held
- information received
- partial
- transferred/referred
- mute refusal
- refusal
- refusal to accept

Argentina: 5, 0, 0, 6, 0, 0, 1, 11, 0, 1

Bulgaria: 0, 4, 2, 10, 0, 0, 5, 3, 0

Mexico: 0, 3, 3, 2, 0, 8, 0, 4, 4

Slovak Republic: 0, 0, 5, 3, 8, 1, 2, 5, 0

South Africa: 0, 2, 0, 5, 0, 0, 13, 4, 0

www.ingramcontent.com/pod-product-compliance
Lightning Source LLC
Chambersburg PA
CBHW080844270326
41929CB00016B/2915